AF322636

American Civil War Trivia

Challenge Your Knowledge with 500 Intriguing Questions and Answers

Welcome Aboard, Check Out This Limited-Time Free Bonus!

Ahoy, reader! Welcome to the Ahoy Publications family, and thanks for snagging a copy of this book! Since you've chosen to join us on this journey, we'd like to offer you something special.

Check out the link below for a FREE e-book filled with delightful facts about American History.

But that's not all - you'll also have access to our exclusive email list with even more free e-books and insider knowledge. Well, what are ye waiting for? Click the link below to join and set sail toward exciting adventures in American History.

Access your bonus here

https://ahoypublications.com/

Or, Scan the QR code!

Table of Contents

Introduction

The American Civil War remains one of the most defining moments in United States history. It was a conflict that drastically changed the course of America and brought us to where we are today.

But how did this devastating war come about? What were its causes, implications, and consequences?

In this trivia book, we will explore these questions and more as we delve into some of the most pivotal events during the Civil War period: from the secession crisis and the Fort Sumter attack in April 1861 to Reconstruction following the Appomattox Court House surrender in April 1865; from the Union blockade impacting Confederate ports for four years to battle strategies driving weapon technology advancements; from the use of photography to document battles across America to African Americans' roles on both sides. No detail is too small or insignificant.

From causes to consequences, leaders to elections, setbacks to successes, and diplomacy to propaganda, each chapter reveals facts you never knew about this war that engrossed the nation.

Are you ready to take a journey through this tumultuous yet defining period of US history? Open this trivia book and get started.

Causes of the American Civil War

The American Civil War was one of the most defining moments of US history and attracted vast attention worldwide. But what were its underlying causes? In this chapter of *American Civil War Trivia*, we will explore the complexities behind how it all began. From disagreements over taxation to growing tensions caused by slavery's expansion and the Fugitive Slave Acts, this collection of trivia questions sheds some light on the core motivators that caused the North and South divide in the early 1860s. Prepare yourself to dig into some fundamental facts about the causes of the American Civil War.

1. **What was the main cause of the American Civil War apart from Lincoln's election?**

    a. The expansion of slavery in states and territories
    b. Economic differences between North and South
    c. Opposition to taxation without representation by the Southern states
    d. Regional differences in cultural values

2. **Which event is considered one of the major catalysts for secession, leading to civil war?**

    a. Battle of Antietam
    b. Dred Scott decision
    c. Compromise of 1850
    d. Kansas-Nebraska Act

3. What document prohibited slavery within certain areas that were part of the United States before 1861?
   a. Proclamation Line of 1763
   b. Emancipation Proclamation
   c. Missouri Compromise
   d. Treaty of Paris

4. Which state was admitted as a slave state after 1820 due to efforts made under the Missouri Compromise?
   a. Kentucky
   b. Texas
   c. California
   d. Missouri

5. What did the Wilmot Proviso suggest as a solution to disputes over slavery in western territories?
   a. Abolish slavery
   b. Grant statehood to slave states
   c. Limit the expansion of slavery
   d. Allowing each territory to decide for itself regarding slavery

6. What was the main reason for increasing political tension between North and South during the 1850s?
   a. Economic differences
   b. Fugitive slave law
   c. Differing views on tariffs
   d. Growing abolitionist movement

7. How did the Tariff of 1828, The "Tariff of Abominations," cause conflict between North and South?
   a. Increased taxes on goods imported by Southern states from Europe
   b. Reduced taxes on US manufactured goods exported to European countries
   c. Depressed prices of agricultural products produced in Southern states
   d. Encouraged industrialization in Northern states

8. **What labor intensive cash crop factored into the war?**
    a. Potatoes
    b. Carrots
    c. Cotton
    d. Tomatoes

9. **What event led to a surge of secessionist movements in the Southern states?**
    a. Abraham Lincoln's election as president
    b. Dred Scott v. Sandford decision
    c. Congress passing new tariff legislation
    d. Abolitionists gaining momentum throughout the US

10. **What did the Fugitive Slave Act of 1850 require?**
    a. All runaway slaves be returned to their owners
    b. Enslaved people serve indefinitely
    c. Slaves be set free in Canada
    d. Killing of runaway slaves on sight

11. **Who proposed the idea of popular sovereignty in Kansas and Nebraska territories, leading to the Bleeding Kansas crisis?**
    a. Abraham Lincoln
    b. Stephen Douglas
    c. John Calhoun
    d. Jefferson Davis

12. **What did the Ostend Manifesto suggest regarding Cuba's annexation by the US?**
    a. Annexation must be done peacefully
    b. The US should purchase Cuba from Spain
    c. The US was morally justified for annexing Cuba with or without Spanish consent
    d. Both B and C

13. **What event led South Carolina to secede from the US?**
    a. Election of Abraham Lincoln
    b. Dred Scott decision
    c. Compromise of 1850
    d. Wilmot Proviso

14. Which region favored tariffs on imported goods more than other regions during the early 1800s?
    a. Northeastern states
    b. Midwestern states
    c. Southern states
    d. Western territories

15. Which state left the Union after Abraham Lincoln's election, making it the first state to secede?
    a. South Carolina
    b. Georgia
    c. Texas
    d. North Carolina

16. What did the Compromise of 1850 attempt to resolve to prevent secession by Southern states?
    a. Expansion of slavery into western territories
    b. Economic disparities between Northern and Southern states
    c. Territorial disputes between Texas and Mexico
    d. Nullification crisis caused by tariffs

17. How did the Dred Scott decision fuel controversy regarding slavery before the Civil War?
    a. It declared free African Americans as citizens with the same rights as white people
    b. It questioned the authority of the federal government over territories owned by the US
    c. It ruled that African Americans were not citizens and that the courts could not recognize cases filed by them at the federal level
    d. It established universal rights for all American citizens regardless of who owned them

18. What happened when Kansas residents voted against the pro-slavery constitution presented by the Lecompton legislature?
    a. It was allowed to become a full-fledged US state
    b. The pro-slavery constitution of Lecompton legislature was enforced
    c. President Buchanan sent federal troops and closed Kansas' pro-slavery government
    d. Kansas's statehood was delayed

19. What previous war created long-lasting ramifications that led to the Civil War?

    a. The War of 1812

    b. The Napoleonic Wars

    c. The Revolutionary War

    d. The Mexican-American War

20. What event occurred just before the Confederate attack on Fort Sumter, South Carolina, and led to the Civil War?

    a. Virginia seceded from the Union

    b. Abraham Lincoln's inaugural address

    c. The Emancipation Proclamation

    d. President Lincoln was assassinated

US Presidential Election of 1860

Join us while we take an exciting journey through the US presidential election of 1860 to uncover some intriguing trivia. Learn about the political parties, presidential candidates, and issues that were significant at this noteworthy time in history. How well do you know your facts? Can you guess who Abraham Lincoln represented during this election or which states did not vote for him? What was John C. Breckinridge's title when he ran in this campaign, and how many electoral votes did President Lincoln receive to win it? Let's find out by testing ourselves with these twenty questions related to the American Civil War.

21. What party did Abraham Lincoln represent in the 1860 US presidential election?
    a. Democratic
    b. Whig
    c. Republican
    d. Populist

22. What was John C. Breckinridge's official title when he ran in this election?
    a. Senator from Kentucky
    b. Vice president of the United States
    c. Governor of California
    d. Secretary of state

23. How many electoral votes did Abraham Lincoln receive to win the election?

    a. 150
    b. 180
    c. 200
    d. 230

24. Who were Abraham Lincoln's opponents in the 1860 US presidential election?

    a. Jefferson Davis and Robert E. Lee
    b. Ulysses S. Grant, Herbert Hoover, and Grover Cleveland
    c. Ross Perot, Ralph Nader, and Jill Stein
    d. John C. Breckinridge, John Bell, and Stephen A. Douglas

25. What issue was most important during this presidential campaign?

    a. Tariffs
    b. Slavery
    c. Immigration
    d. Education reform

26. How many states were in the Union at that time of the election?

    a. Twenty-four
    b. Twenty-six
    c. Twenty-eight
    d. Thirty-three

27. Which state did not vote for Abraham Lincoln in this election?

    a. Pennsylvania
    b. South Carolina
    c. Massachusetts
    d. New York

28. Who won both the popular vote and the Electoral College votes?

    a. Stephen Douglas
    b. John Bell
    c. John C. Breckinridge
    d. Abraham Lincoln

29. What was the name of the Constitutional Union Party's candidate in this election?
   a. Abraham Lincoln
   b. Stephen Douglas
   c. William Seward
   d. John Bell

30. Who was not one of the candidates in this election?
   a. James Buchanan
   b. John Bell
   c. Stephen Douglas
   d. John C. Breckinridge

31. What did Abraham Lincoln promise to do if elected president?
   a. End slavery
   b. Increase tariffs
   c. Reinstate states' rights
   d. Abolish education reform

32. How many electoral votes were needed to win the 1860 US presidential election?
   a. 152
   b. 180
   c. 200
   d. 230

33. Which candidate represented the Southern Democratic Party during this election?
   a. William Seward
   b. Abraham Lincoln
   c. Stephen Douglas
   d. John C. Breckinridge

34. What political party did most Southern states vote for in this election?
   a. Democratic
   b. Republican
   c. Whig
   d. Unionist

35. **What was Abraham Lincoln's main campaign slogan during this election?**
    a. "Free soil, free speech, free labor and free men"
    b. "A house divided against itself cannot stand"
    c. "Vote for change"
    d. "Vote yourself a farm and horses"

36. **How was Lincoln informed of his nomination as candidate for the Republican Party for the 1860 presidential election?**
    a. Telephone
    b. Telegram
    c. Instagram
    d. Word of mouth

37. **What western states cast their electoral votes for Abraham Lincoln during the 1860 election?**
    a. Nevada and Arizona
    b. California and Oregon
    c. Utah and Montana
    d. Idaho

38. **South Carolina seceded from the Union after the 1860 US presidential election—what happened next?**
    a. Other Southern states followed suit
    b. Northern states declared war
    c. President-elect Abraham Lincoln called for peace talks
    d. Outgoing US President James Buchanan declared martial law

39. **Why did the Constitutional Union Party nominate John Bell as their presidential candidate?**
    a. He was an experienced politician
    b. He was against the expansion of slavery
    c. He wanted to preserve the Union
    d. All the above

40. **Who became vice president when Abraham Lincoln won this election?**
    a. Stephen Douglas
    b. Hannibal Hamlin
    c. Andrew Johnson
    d. William Seward

The Secession of Southern States

The American Civil War was a bloody conflict that rocked the nation in the mid-nineteenth century. During this time, many states seceded from the Union to form their own country, which became known as the "Confederacy." The secession of Southern states is an important part of America's history, and it has left us with some fascinating trivia to explore. In this chapter, we'll be examining questions about why these states seceded from the Union and what events caused them to do so. We'll also learn facts about who wrote "South Carolina Exposition and Protest," when each Confederate state declared itself a part of the Confederacy during secession, and why some border slaveholding states initially refused to join forces with other Southern states. So, let's dive into these American Civil War trivia questions.

41. **How many Confederate states seceded from the Union, leading to the Civil War?**
    a. Four states
    b. Five states
    c. Six states
    d. Eleven states

42. **When did South Carolina officially become a member state of the Confederacy?**
    a. December 21, 1860
    b. May 20, 1861
    c. April 12, 1861
    d. February 8, 1861

43. Which state was not among those Who declared themselves part of the Confederacy during secession?

    a. Virginia
    b. Georgia
    c. Mississippi
    d. Delaware

44. Why were some slaveholding border states like Kentucky and Maryland reluctant to join other Southern states when they seceded?

    a. They feared negative economic consequences
    b. They feared the Union would retaliate
    c. They did not agree with slavery
    d. Both a and b

45. What amendment was passed in 1865 that abolished slavery?

    a. The Thirteenth Amendment
    b. The Fourteenth Amendment
    c. The Fifteenth Amendment
    d. The Sixteenth Amendment

46. Who wrote "South Carolina Exposition and Protest," which argued for state sovereignty and against an unconstitutional central government?

    a. John C. Calhoun
    b. Andrew Jackson
    c. Thomas Jefferson
    d. Abraham Lincoln

47. Why were Southern states so keen on seceding from the Union before 1860?

    a. To form their own nation based on slave labor
    b. To protest federal tariffs imposed by President James Madison
    c. To protect themselves from foreign aggression
    d. To expand their political power in other regions of the country

48. Which Confederate state had its secession declared illegal by President Abraham Lincoln?
    a. Virginia
    b. South Carolina
    c. Mississippi
    d. Texas

49. What was the last state to join the Confederacy in 1861?
    a. Tennessee
    b. Alabama
    c. North Carolina
    d. Arkansas

50. How long did it take for all eleven Confederate states to secede from the Union?
    a. Less than one month
    b. Three months
    c. Six months
    d. Nine months

51. What document declared that the secession of individual states was illegal and unconstitutional?
    a. The Emancipation Proclamation
    b. The Compromise of 1850
    c. The Declaration of Independence
    d. The Articles of Confederation

52. Why did some Southern militia groups resist federal troops sent into their territories during secession?
    a. To prevent abolitionists from entering their territory
    b. To protect themselves against outside aggression
    c. To defend their right to own slaves
    d. To oppose President Lincoln's efforts to preserve the Union

53. Who wrote "Declaration of the Immediate Causes Which Induce and Justify the Secession," which argued for the secession of individual states from the Union?
    a. John C. Calhoun
    b. Robert E. Lee
    c. Christopher G. Memminger
    d. Benjamin F. Arthur

54. **When did South Carolina become the first state to secede from the Union?**
    a. December 20, 1860
    b. December 10, 1861
    c. April 12, 1861
    d. May 9, 1860

55. **What did Southern politicians attempt during secession, as they feared losing their slaves if they remained part of the United States?**
    a. To create new slave-owning territories
    b. To pass legislation banning slavery within the Confederacy's boundaries
    c. To negotiate trade deals with foreign nations for more slaves
    d. To offer financial compensation to former slaveholders

56. **What did President Abraham Lincoln do in response to the Confederate states seceding from the Union?**
    a. He declared war on them
    b. He issued an executive order
    c. He offered negotiations for peace
    d. He imposed martial law

57. **During secession, What was the name given to federal troops sent into the Southern States by President Abraham Lincoln?**
    a. The Secessionists
    b. The Rebels
    c. The Confederates
    d. The Union Army

58. **Who was elected as president of the Confederate States of America?**
    a. James Buchanan
    b. John Bell
    c. Jefferson Davis
    d. Thomas Jefferson

59. What was the initial response of the Confederate States of America to Abraham Lincoln's 1861 proclamation that declared an end to secession?

   a. Jefferson Davis challenged Abraham Lincoln to a duel
   b. They offered negotiations for peace
   c. They imposed martial law
   d. They ignored it

60. In what year did Mississippi become a Confederate state after it signed its Ordinance of Secession?

   a. 1859
   b. 1861
   c. 1862
   d. 1865

Fort Sumter Attack and Surrender

The beginning of the American Civil War was marked by a tumultuous event: the Battle of Fort Sumter. A relatively small fort strategically situated offshore from Charleston became the center of attention as Confederate forces opened fire against Union troops stationed inside. Questions quickly arise: Who commanded each side during this battle? How much damage was inflicted on both sides due to the poor strategies employed in the battle? These answers (and more) will be uncovered when you delve into this chapter. From how Confederate Major General Pierre G. T. Beauregard concocted his military plan of attack to President Lincoln's response—hidden nuggets of information are ready to be discovered.

61.   **What was the date of the attack on Fort Sumter?**
   a.   April 12, 1861
   b.   April 11, 1861
   c.   April 13, 1861
   d.   April 14, 1861

62.   **Who commanded the Confederate forces during the battle?**
   a.   General Pierre G. T. Beauregard
   b.   General Robert E. Lee
   c.   General Ulysses S. Grant
   d.   General Thomas J. Jackson

63. **How long did this battle last?**
    a. One hour and thirty minutes
    b. Three hours and fifteen minutes
    c. Thirty-four hours
    d. Six hours and ten minutes

64. **Why were Union troops in Fort Sumter attacked by Confederate soldiers in April 1861?**
    a. Confederates claimed ownership of the fort and considered attempts to resupply the fort an affront to state sovereignty
    b. The Confederates accused the Union troops of harassing locals
    c. To demonstrate Southern resolve against the Union forces
    d. To protect Charleston from an enemy invasion

65. **Who fired the first shots of Fort Sumter?**
    a. Confederate troops
    b. Union troops
    c. Locals from Charleston
    d. Ulysses S. Grant

66. **How many casualties were there on both sides during this battle?**
    a. Zero
    b. Ten
    c. Twenty
    d. Fifty

67. **What was General Beauregard's plan for taking control of Fort Sumter?**
    a. A full-scale assault
    b. A siege to starve out defenders
    c. Bombardment from Confederate artillery
    d. An ultimatum demanding surrender

68. **Where did President Jefferson Davis establish his headquarters before the attack on Fort Sumter?**
    a. Montgomery, Alabama
    b. Washington, D.C.
    c. Richmond, Virginia
    d. Charleston, South Carolina

69. **What Union soldier switched sides to the Confederates after the fall of Fort Sumter?**

   a. Stonewall Jackson
   b. Johnny Cash Machine
   c. Robert E. Lee
   d. Richard Kidder Meade

70. **What was the primary response from President Lincoln to the Confederate fire on Fort Sumter?**

   a. He issued a proclamation calling for 75,000 volunteers
   b. He ordered an immediate counterattack
   c. He demanded surrender
   d. He offered peace negotiations

71. **Who ultimately surrendered control of Fort Sumter in April 1861?**

   a. Major Robert Anderson
   b. General Robert E. Lee
   c. General Pierre G. T. Beauregard
   d. Colonel Abner Doubleday

72. **How much damage did the bombardment cause to Fort Sumter during the battle?**

   a. Complete destruction
   b. No damage
   c. Moderate damage
   d. Minor damage

73. **Who was responsible for delivering supplies to Fort Sumter while it was under siege?**

   a. The US Navy
   b. Confederate forces
   c. Local Charleston merchants
   d. Union troops from other states

74. **From Where was the first shot fired at Fort Sumter?**

   a. An artillery battery located on James Island
   b. Look Out Mountain
   c. A tree
   d. The deck of Beauregard's ship

75. **What were some reasons Major Robert Anderson cited in his message to President Lincoln after his surrender at Fort Sumter?**

   a. Anderson himself was deathly ill
   b. Most of his troops had switched sides
   c. They were running low on food and ammunition
   d. Too many people were being killed

76. **How many days did it take for Union reinforcements to reach Fort Sumter during the battle?**

   a. Four
   b. Two
   c. Six
   d. They never made it

77. **What was General Beauregard's response when Major Robert Anderson refused his surrender terms?**

   a. He sent another ultimatum demanding immediate evacuation
   a. He threatened an invasion of Washington, D.C.
   b. He offered additional supplies in exchange for surrender
   c. He fired on the fort

78. **What message did President Lincoln deliver after news of Fort Sumter's fall reached him?**

   a. A proclamation declaring war against the Confederate states
   b. A call to arms
   c. Acceptance and praise for the Confederacy
   d. An offer of peace negotiations

79. **What was the final result of the battle?**

   a. Both sides reached a stalemate, resulting in a surrender agreement
   b. The fort's walls were breached by Union troops
   c. The Confederate forces retreated after realizing their inferior firepower
   d. The Union forces were defeated and evacuated Fort Sumter

First Battle of Bull Run/Manassas

Early optimism and harsh reality collided at the First Battle of Bull Run. What many on both sides expected to be a quick and decisive clash instead became a chaotic test of leadership, preparation, and resolve. Just outside Washington, inexperienced Union and Confederate armies met for the first major land battle of the war, drawing soldiers, generals, and even curious civilians into a confrontation that would shatter illusions of an easy victory. From flawed battle plans to the moment the tide turned, this section asks questions about the clash that proved the Civil War would be longer—and bloodier—than anyone imagined.

80. **On What date did the First Battle of Bull Run/Manassas take place?**
    a. June 21, 1861
    b. July 16, 1863
    c. July 21, 1861
    d. September 17, 1862

81. **Who commanded Confederate forces at the First Battle of Bull Run/Manassas?**
    a. Robert E. Lee
    b. Ulysses S. Grant
    c. Thomas J. Jackson
    d. P.G.T. Beauregard

82. How many Union soldiers were killed in action during the engagement at the First Battle of Bull Run?

   a. 3,200
   b. 4,500
   c. 6,200
   d. 450–700

83. Which Southern state is closest to the battlefield site for the First Battle of Bull Run/Manassas?

   a. North Carolina
   b. South Carolina
   c. Virginia
   d. Georgia

84. What elected official was taken as a prisoner of war during the First Battle of Bull Run/Manassas?

   a. Chicago Mayor Richard Daley
   b. Republican Congressman Alfred Ely
   c. Secretary of War William Henry Seward
   d. Whig Senator Henry Clay

85. Who was in command of the Army of Northeastern Virginia at the start of the battle?

   a. P.G.T. Beauregard and Joseph E. Johnston
   b. Winfield Scott
   c. Joseph E. Johnston
   d. Robert E. Lee

86. Which of these was not a factor in the early victory for the Confederates at the First Battle of Bull Run?

   a. Confederate forces had better military tactics than their counterparts
   b. The terrain favored defense over offense
   c. Union troops lacked training
   d. Confederates had more supplies than Union troops

87. **What was an infamous mishap from an Associated Press reporter who covered the First Battle of Bull Run?**

    a. Being mistaken for a spy by the advancing Confederate forces

    b. Getting shot and killed while covering the story

    c. Leaving a camera on the front lines, thereby allowing valuable intel to fall into Confederate hands

    d. Making an early exit to report a Union victory, only to later learn of the defeat

88. **Which Confederate general gained fame from his performance during the First Battle of Bull Run/Manassas?**

    a. Robert E. Lee

    b. Thomas J. Jackson

    c. Ulysses S. Grant

    d. George B. McClellan

89. **How many brigades were in Beauregard's command at the start of the battle?**

    a. Seven

    b. Four

    c. Five

    d. Three

90. **Where did General McDowell begin his march toward Richmond before engaging in battle with Confederate forces?**

    a. Centreville

    b. Manassas Junction

    c. Bull's Gap

    d. Washington, D.C.

91. **Who won control of Henry House Hill following fierce fighting during the battle?**

    a. Confederate forces

    b. Union forces

    c. Neither side won control of it

    d. Both sides had equal claim to it

92. **What was the original intended goal for McDowell's march on Manassas (First Battle)?**
   a. To seize Manassas railroad junction
   b. To outflank Confederate positions in Richmond
   c. To engage and overwhelm Beauregard's troops
   d. To capture Beauregard

93. **Who were some well-known Union generals Who took part in the First Battle of Bull Run?**
   a. Irvin McDowell, William T. Sherman, James Longstreet
   b. Joseph E. Johnston, Thomas J. Jackson, Robert E. Lee
   c. Winfield Scott, Ulysses S. Grant, P.G.T. Beauregard
   d. James Longstreet, Ambrose Burnside, Joseph Hooker

94. **How many days did it take for reinforcements from both sides to reach the battlefield?**
   a. One day
   b. Two days
   c. Three days
   d. Four days

95. **Who ordered McDowell's troops to withdraw from Centreville and re-group with other forces further north of Bull Run Creek?**
   a. Winfield Scott
   b. Joseph E. Johnston
   c. Irvin McDowell
   d. Robert E. Lee

96. **What was the primary strategy used by Confederate forces during the First Battle of Bull Run?**
   a. Attack and overwhelm Union troops with superior numbers
   b. Defend territory while waiting for reinforcements
   c. Cut off Union supply lines
   d. Outflank Union positions

97. **Who started referring to General Thomas J. Jackson as "Stonewall" Jackson during the battle?**
   a. Jefferson Davis
   b. Union General George B. McClellan
   c. Confederate General Bernard Bee
   d. Abraham Lincoln

98. Who were some of the well-known Confederate generals Who took part in the First Battle of Bull Run?

   a. Thomas J. Jackson, Bernard Bee, Joseph Johnston
   b. Ulysses S. Grant, PGT Beauregard, Winfield Scott
   c. James Longstreet, Ambrose Burnside, Joseph Hooker
   d. Irvin McDowell, William T. Sherman, George B. McClellan

99. Why is the First Battle of Bull Run/Manassas significant in American history?

   a. It was the first major land battle of the Civil War
   b. It was an early victory for Confederate forces
   c. It marked a turning point in Union strategy and tactics
   d. It demonstrated that Confederate troops could stand up to Union forces

Union Blockade of Confederate Ports

As one of the most significant military struggles fought on United States soil, the Union blockade of Confederate ports shaped the course of events throughout the American Civil War. Delve into trivia that encompasses battle strategy, weapon technology innovation, naval blockades along the Southern coast, and diplomatic missions abroad with foreign powers for aid or assistance. Explore the fascinating stories of privateers who took immense risks running contraband goods past threatening ships at sea and uncover vivid accounts and details of Union soldiers' experiences while living on blockade runners. Find out why this was a defining moment in history that marked an irrevocable boundary between Northern and Southern states. Get ready to pose your hypothesis after learning what made this conflict so incredibly unique.

100. **What was the main purpose of the Union blockade of Confederate ports during the Civil War?**
    a. To block Confederate exports and prevent supplies from entering Confederate territory
    b. To keep European powers out of the conflict
    c. To limit trade between North and South
    d. To pressure President Jefferson Davis to surrender

101.   How many years did this blockade last?
   a.   One
   b.   Two
   c.   Three
   d.   Four

102.   What was the first Union ship to blockade a Southern seaport?
   a.   USS Nimitz
   b.   USS Saratoga
   c.   The Good Ship Lollypop
   d.   USS *Niagara*

103.   What type of vessels were used by both sides to break through naval blockades to run contraband goods?
   a.   Submarines
   b.   Merchant ships
   c.   Naval warships
   d.   Aircraft carriers

104.   In what year was Congress granted the authority to use a naval blockade of Confederate ports?
   a.   1861
   b.   1862
   c.   1863
   d.   1864

105.   What was the most successful Southern seaport for blockade runners?
   a.   New Orleans, Louisiana
   b.   Daytona, Florida
   c.   Muncie, Indiana
   d.   Wilmington, North Carolina

106.   How did European powers respond to the Union blockade during the Civil War?
   a.   They provided military assistance to help break it down
   b.   They supplied arms and ammunition to both sides
   c.   They supported efforts by North and South alike
   d.   They remained neutral, refusing involvement in US affairs

107. Which areas were affected by an embargo imposed upon exports from Confederate states due to their secession from the Union?

    a. Agricultural products
    b. Manufactured goods
    c. Raw materials
    d. All the above

108. In what year did Congress pass a law that allowed the Union to purchase ships and enlist their privateers?

    a. 1861
    b. 1862
    c. 1863
    d. 1864

109. What strategic plan did the Union blockade form a central part of during the Civil War?

    a. The Gettysburg Campaign
    b. The Overland Campaign
    c. The Anaconda Plan
    d. The Peninsula Campaign

110. What were some methods used by blockade runners to evade detection from the Union Navy during the Civil War?

    a. Changing course quickly
    b. Flying flags of neutral countries
    c. Running at night with no lights
    d. All the above

111. Which state had the most ports that were blockaded by Union forces during the Civil War?

    a. Virginia
    b. Georgia
    c. South Carolina
    d. Florida

112. Why did many vessels choose not to comply with the Union blockade during the Civil War?

    a. They feared reprisal from Confederate forces
    b. Though risky, it was profitable to get supplies into Confederate territories
    c. The cost of complying with the blockade was too high
    d. All the above

113. How many blockade runners commanded by Confederate naval
     officers were captured during the war?

     a. six
     b. none
     c. ten
     d. four

114. How did some states attempt to break through Union blockades
     to bring needed goods and materials into Southern ports?

     a. By constructing ironclad ships
     b. By using blockade runners
     c. By sending diplomatic missions abroad
     d. By negotiating trade agreements with foreign powers

115. How did the Union Navy respond to vessels attempting to break
     through their naval blockades?

     a. By destroying the ships
     b. By seizing contraband
     c. By imprisoning crew members
     d. All the above

116. What military action cut off Wilmington, North Carolina as a
     blockade-running port?

     a. The port was bombarded
     b. Union capture of Fort Fisher on January 15, 1865, cut off
         the port
     c. Port authorities declared martial law
     d. Union troops cut off the water supply

117. Where did the Union blockade begin in 1861?

     a. Charleston Harbor, South Carolina
     b. Norfolk Harbor, Virginia
     c. Mobile Bay, Alabama
     d. Port Royal Sound, South Carolina

118. Which type of ships were excluded by President Lincoln's
     proclamation announcing an effective Union blockade?

     a. None
     b. Sailboats
     c. Steamers
     d. Fishing vessels

119. Which type of ships were used by both sides to break through the Union blockade during the Civil War?

   a. Submarines
   b. Destroyers
   c. Side-wheel steamers
   d. Cruisers

Battle of Antietam and Emancipation Proclamation

Experience one of the most decisive moments in American history with these questions about the Battle of Antietam and the Emancipation Proclamation. Delve into this important chapter to test your knowledge on topics such as Union commanders, Confederate objectives, casualties sustained during battle, and technology used. Get ready!

120. **What proclamation did President Lincoln issue right after the Battle of Antietam?**

   a. Proclamation of victory

   b. Proclamation of a national draft

   c. The Emancipation Proclamation

   d. Proclamation of a national Antietam Day of Remembrance

121. **When did President Abraham Lincoln issue the Emancipation Proclamation?**

   a. July 4, 1863

   b. January 1, 1863

   c. November 5, 1862

   d. September 22, 1862

122. **Who commanded Union troops during the Battle of Antietam?**

   a. Ulysses S. Grant

   b. Robert E. Lee

   c. Joseph Hooker

   d. George B. McClellan

123. How many casualties were sustained by both sides at the Battle of Antietam?

   a. 13,000
   b. 23,000
   c. 33,000
   d. 43,000

124. What effect did the Emancipation Proclamation have on African American slaves?

   a. Slaves within Confederate states were declared free
   b. It declared that all enslaved people in Confederate states must be returned to their owners
   c. Slaves were declared free citizens with full rights
   d. It gave them the right to vote

125. After Harpers Ferry fell to Stonewall Jackson, during the Battle of Antietam, what weapons were confiscated?

   a. 13,000 small arms and 73 cannons
   b. 50 grenades and 20 bazookas
   c. 100 rifles and 554 muskets
   d. 75 muskets, 24 swords, and 2 sling shots

126. How many days did the Battle of Antietam last?

   a. One day
   b. Seven days
   c. Ten days
   d. Fourteen days

127. Who issued the preliminary version of the Emancipation Proclamation in 1862?

   a. Abraham Lincoln
   b. Ulysses S. Grant
   c. George B. McClellan
   d. Robert E. Lee

128. What other name was the battle of Antietam known by?

   a. Battle of Bigfoot
   b. Battle of Sharpsburg
   c. Battle of Wounded Knee
   d. Beat 'Em at Antietam

129. What was the purpose of the Emancipation Proclamation?
   a. To declare war on the Confederate states
   b. To end slavery in America
   c. To gain support for the Union cause
   d. To seek foreign intervention against the Confederacy

130. About how many troops did General Robert E. Lee command during the Battle of Antietam?
   a. 10,000
   b. 18,000
   c. 30,000
   d. 40,000

131. What was the significance of the Battle of Antietam?
   a. It secured Union victory
   b. It resulted in a complete Confederate victory
   c. It was the first battle fought on United States soil
   d. It was a tactical draw that enabled the Emancipation Proclamation to be issued and enforced

132. Who commanded Confederate forces at the Battle of Antietam?
   a. Ulysses S. Grant
   b. Robert E. Lee
   c. Joseph Hooker
   d. George B. McClellan

133. When was the preliminary version of the Emancipation Proclamation signed?
   a. November 5, 1862
   b. January 1, 1863
   c. July, 1863
   d. September 22, 1862

134. President Lincoln was first prompted to issue the preliminary Emancipation when General McClellan mistakenly did what at the Battle of Antietam?
   a. Declared a Union victory
   b. Declared a Confederate victory
   c. Declared a stalemate
   d. Sought international intervention

135. **Who was the main commander of Union forces during the Battle of Antietam?**

a. Ulysses S. Grant
b. Robert E. Lee
c. Joseph Hooker
d. George B. McClellan

136. **When did the Battle of Antietam take place?**

a. July 4, 1862
b. August 15, 1862
c. September 17, 1862
d. November 5, 1862

137. **How did General Robert E. Lee's decision to cross into Maryland contribute to the Battle of Antietam?**

a. It allowed him access to more supplies and resources
b. It brought his army closer to Washington, D.C., providing a strategic advantage
c. It encouraged volunteer enlistments in support of secessionist forces
d. It provided an opportunity for Confederate troops to attack Union troops without warning

138. **In what way was new technology used during the battle at Antietam?**

a. Massive airships were developed capable of dropping bombs on enemy positions
b. Mustard gas was deployed in battle
c. Hand grenades were thrown
d. Telegraph wires were used to send messages between army headquarters

139. **What was one of General Robert E. Lee's primary goals in invading Maryland in 1862?**

a. To gain enough supplies and support from the local population for a successful conquest of Washington, D.C.
b. To demonstrate Union military weakness by taking control of strategic points along the border with Pennsylvania
c. To boost Confederate morale by engaging in a battle outside Confederate territory
d. To create an independent nation separate from both North and South without relying on foreign aid

Draft Riots in the North

The long, bitter conflict left lasting scars on both the North and South, but some of the most painful wounds of this turbulent period were experienced by those living in Northern cities. One such event was the draft riots, which took place throughout the Northern states. This chapter will explore these riots—who instigated them, what they looked like on the ground, how long they lasted, and their ultimate consequences. Come along as we unravel a tangled web of economic grievances fueled by racial angst to uncover why there were draft riots in America during one of its darkest times.

140. **What year did the draft riots in the North take place?**
    a. 1862
    b. 1863
    c. 1864
    d. 1865

141. **About how long did the riots last?**
    a. Nearly a week
    b. Two months
    c. Half a year
    d. Four hours

142. **Who instigated the draft riots of July 1863 in the North?**
    a. African Americans
    b. Abolitionists
    c. Politicians
    d. The poor white working-class

143. **Where were most of the rioters from, geographically speaking?**
    a. The South
    b. The Midwest
    c. New York City
    d. Rural areas near Rochester

144. **How were members of Irish-American communities affected by this event?**
    a. They mostly remained neutral
    b. They supported it actively
    c. They suffered disproportionately
    d. They benefited economically

145. **Which group was targeted during these riots and why?**
    a. African Americans, because of their employment status
    b. Poor whites, because of the cost of conscription
    c. Politicians, to create chaos and instability
    d. Northern laborers, as scapegoats

146. **What event caused a large wave of immigration from Ireland before the riots?**
    a. The Potato Famine
    b. The Great Migration
    c. The American Revolution
    d. World War I

147. **How did President Lincoln respond to the draft riots in the North?**
    a. He sent Union troops
    b. He issued pardons
    c. He imposed martial law
    d. He declared an amnesty

148. **What role did the "Peace Democrats" play in the draft riots?**
    a. They organized and led the riots as a coordinated national movement
    b. They opposed the Civil War and encouraged resistance to the draft
    c. They supported the draft but protested how it was enforced
    d. They attempted to suppress the riots in cooperation with Union authorities

149. **Which groups were most likely to join forces during this event?**
    a. Irish immigrants and African Americans
    b. Rich merchants and poor laborers
    c. Pro-Unionists and Confederate sympathizers
    d. Native New Yorkers and recent arrivals

150. **To what degree was public order restored by July 1863?**
    a. Completely restored
    b. Partially restored
    c. Not at all restored
    d. Temporarily suspended

151. **Who acted as the primary mediators between the rioters and local government forces?**
    a. Politicians
    b. Government soldiers
    c. Civilians
    d. No one

152. **What is one of the most significant legacies of this event?**
    a. The rise of organized labor
    b. The end of slavery in America
    c. Heightened racial tensions
    d. Greater solidarity among immigrants

153. **How did New York City handle these riots?**
    a. By imposing martial law
    b. By establishing curfews
    c. By deploying police units
    d. All the above

154. **What were some immediate consequences for those arrested during these riots?**
    a. Imprisonment
    b. Death sentences
    c. Forced conscription into military service
    d. Deportation to foreign countries

155. Which groups benefited from the draft riots in the North, if any?

   a. African Americans
   b. Poor whites
   c. Rich merchants
   d. None of the above

156. What did the riots reveal about government policies at that time?

   a. They were largely ineffective
   b. They were too lenient
   c. They favored certain groups
   d. All the above

157. Who was ultimately responsible for restoring order in New York City after these riots?

   a. The federal government
   b. Local politicians
   c. Private citizens
   d. Military forces

158. How many people were convicted of riot-related crimes during this period?

   a. 40
   b. 100
   c. 67
   d. 400

159. How did public opinion regarding conscription change as a result of these riots?

   a. It became more favorable
   b. It became less favorable
   c. It remained unchanged
   d. It increased drastically

Battle of Chickamauga and Battle of Nashville

Take a journey with us through the American Civil War to answer some of history's most intriguing questions about two of the war's greatest battles: the Battle of Chickamauga and the Battle of Nashville. From commanders to strategies and casualties to outcomes, test your knowledge on these bloody battlefields as we seek out fascinating facts about each battle. Dive deep into the past as you work through this trivia, covering important moments in America's past during this famed civil war.

160.   Who was the Union commander at the Battle of Chickamauga?
   a.   General William Rosecrans
   b.   Thomas J. "Stonewall" Jackson
   c.   Ulysses S. Grant
   d.   William T. Sherman

161.   Where did the Battle of Nashville take place?
   a.   Tennessee
   b.   Georgia
   c.   Alabama
   d.   Mississippi

162. **What occurred during the first day of fighting in Chattanooga?**

   a. Confederate forces retreated from Lookout Mountain and Missionary Ridge

   b. The Union Army drove Confederate forces out of Chattanooga

   c. Union forces surrounded Confederates on Orchard Knob

   d. The armies began skirmishing around Horseshoe Ridge

163. **When were both battles at Chattanooga fought?**

   a. 1861-62

   b. 1862-63

   c. 1863-64

   d. 1864-65

164. **Who won the Battle of Nashville?**

   a. The Confederacy

   b. The Union

   c. Neither side won

   d. Both sides won

165. **What was the Confederate strategy during the Battle of Chickamauga?**

   a. To surround and trap Union forces

   b. To draw out the battle by attacking at multiple points

   c. To utilize their overwhelming numerical superiority to overwhelm Union forces

   d. To retreat until reinforcements could arrive

166. **General Longstreet arrived to reinforce the Confederates at Chickamauga, but he had to find them first. How did he get there?**

   a. He simply followed the sounds of battle

   b. He employed GPS

   c. He relied on smoke signals

   d. He followed coordinates sent from telegraph stations

167. **Who commanded the Army of Tennessee during the Battle of Nashville?**

   a. Braxton Bragg

   b. William T. Sherman

   c. Philip Sheridan

   d. John Bell Hood

168. How long did it take for the Army of Tennessee to move from Atlanta to Nashville?

    a. Two weeks

    b. One month

    c. Two months

    d. Three months

169. What was the purpose of General Bragg's offensive maneuvers at Chickamauga?

    a. To draw out Union forces from Chattanooga

    b. To encircle and trap Union forces in Chattanooga

    c. To retake strategic points along the Tennessee River

    d. To prevent reinforcements from reaching Nashville

170. Who commanded Confederate troops during the Battle of Chickamauga?

    a. Robert E. Lee

    b. Braxton Bragg

    c. Nathan Bedford Forrest

    d. John Bell Hood

171. What strategic railroad ran in close proximity to Tennessee's Cumberland River?

    a. The Pony Express

    b. The Louisville and Nashville

    c. The Union Pacific

    d. Amtrak

172. Who won the Battle of Chickamauga?

    a. The Union

    b. Neither side won

    c. The Confederacy

    d. Both sides won

173. Where did most of the fighting at the Battle of Nashville take place?

    a. At Orchard Knob

    b. In the hills outside of Chattanooga

    c. Along the Cumberland River

    d. On Missionary Ridge

174. **What happened to Confederate forces after their defeat in the Battle of Nashville?**
   a. They retreated to Alabama
   b. They were surrounded by Union troops
   c. They were forced into surrender
   d. They regrouped and counter-attacked

175. **When did the fighting in Nashville begin?**
   a. December 15, 1864
   b. November 25, 1863
   c. September 21, 1862
   d. August 24, 1865

176. **Who commanded Union forces during the Battle of Chickamauga?**
   a. William T. Sherman
   b. Braxton Bragg
   c. George Thomas
   d. Philip Sheridan

177. **What was General Hood's strategy at the Battle of Nashville?**
   a. To retreat until reinforcements could arrive
   b. To draw out battle by attacking at multiple points
   c. To surround and trap Union forces
   d. To utilize their overwhelming numerical superiority to overwhelm Union forces

178. **How many casualties occurred in the Battle of Chickamauga?**
   a. Less than 10,000
   b. Between 10,000 and 20,000
   c. More than 50,000
   d. Around 30,000

179. **Who commanded the Army of the Cumberland during the Battle of Nashville?**
   a. Braxton Bragg
   b. William T. Sherman
   c. Philip Sheridan
   d. George Thomas

Gettysburg Address Delivered by Lincoln

From the bloodiest battle of the American Civil War came one of history's most prominent speeches. The Gettysburg Address delivered by Lincoln has become a cornerstone in US history. The depth of emotion behind these lines not only shaped public opinion for years to come but also inspired creative expression and patriotic thought. This chapter explores numerous trivia questions related to Abraham Lincoln's iconic Gettysburg Address, ranging from the date it was given to the original stories or people who underpinned it.

180.   **When was the Gettysburg Address delivered by Lincoln?**
    a.   1863
    b.   1864
    c.   1865
    d.   1861

181.   **How long did it take for Lincoln to deliver his address at Gettysburg?**
    a.   One hour
    b.   Two minutes
    c.   Five minutes
    d.   Ten seconds

182. **What was not included in the speech made by Abraham Lincoln at Gettysburg?**
   a. A call for the end of slavery
   b. An appeal to civil justice
   c. A tribute to fallen soldiers
   d. Quotes from ancient literature

183. **Where was the site of the battle that is remembered through the words of President Abraham Lincoln's famous speech?**
   a. Antietam, Maryland
   b. Bull Run, Virginia
   c. Fort Sumter, South Carolina
   d. Gettysburg, Pennsylvania

184. **Who wrote the lyrics of the "Battle Hymn of the Republic," which inspired President Abraham?**
   a. Julia Ward Howe
   b. Henry Wadsworth Longfellow
   c. William Wordsworth
   d. Walt Whitman

185. **In which state is Gettysburg located?**
   a. Pennsylvania
   b. Virginia
   c. Maryland
   d. New Jersey

186. **How many sentences were included in the Gettysburg Address by President Abraham Lincoln?**
   a. Four
   b. Five
   c. Ten
   d. Fifteen

187. **What was the main purpose of Lincoln's address at Gettysburg?**
   a. To inspire patriotism and national unity
   b. To call for an end to slavery
   c. To declare war on the Confederate states
   d. To honor fallen soldiers from both sides

188. **Who wrote the Gettysburg Address?**
   a. Thomas Jefferson
   b. William Henry Seward
   c. Ulysses S. Grant
   d. Abraham Lincoln

189. **How did President Abraham Lincoln begin his speech at Gettysburg?**
   a. "Four score and seven years ago"
   b. "We have gathered here today"
   c. "Our fathers brought forth on this continent"
   d. "Let us never forget our duty"

190. **What is the most quoted line in the Gettysburg Address?**
   a. "Four score and seven years ago"
   b. "We have met the enemy and they are ours"
   c. "From these honored dead we take increased devotion to that cause for which they gave their last full measure of devotion"
   d. "Let us never forget our duty"

191. **Who was not present at President Abraham Lincoln's speech at Gettysburg?**
   a. Ulysses S. Grant
   b. Jefferson Davis
   c. Robert E. Lee
   d. All the above

192. **How did President Abraham Lincoln conclude his address at Gettysburg?**
   a. With quotes from ancient literature
   b. By calling for an end to slavery
   c. With inspiring words about freedom
   d. With reminders of historical context

193. **What larger idea did Lincoln link the Civil War to in the Gettysburg Address?**
   a. The preservation of the Union as originally formed
   b. The principles of equality expressed in the Declaration of Independence
   c. The military superiority of the Union Army
   d. The economic future of the Northern states

194. How many words were included in the Gettysburg Address by President Abraham Lincoln?

    a. 10
    b. 250
    c. 300
    d. 272

195. What audience did Lincoln say could not truly dedicate or consecrate the battlefield at Gettysburg?

    a. The United States Congress
    b. The citizens attending the ceremony
    c. The soldiers who fought in the battle
    d. The clergy present at the dedication

196. Who was Abraham Lincoln addressing with his speech at Gettysburg?

    a. Confederate states
    b. Union Army officers
    c. American citizens
    d. Fallen soldiers from both sides

197. What memorial was erected at Gettysburg to remember the fallen soldiers?

    a. Antietam Memorial
    b. Freedom Monument
    c. Lincoln Memorial
    d. Soldiers' National Cemetery

198. In what month was the Gettysburg Address delivered by Lincoln?

    a. January
    b. April
    c. November
    d. August

199. About how long after the battle at Gettysburg did President Lincoln deliver his address?

    a. One year
    b. Two weeks
    c. Four years
    d. Four and a half months

The Overland Campaign in Virginia

The Overland Campaign in Virginia was one of the most significant military campaigns ever to take place on American soil. Thousands of brave men were sacrificed during this time, some in decisive battles and others in drawn-out engagements in which neither side made significant gains or losses. Test your knowledge about this grueling war by answering our questions and unraveling the secrets behind one of America's greatest Civil War trials—the Overland Campaign.

200. When did the Overland Campaign in Virginia take place?
    a. 1861
    b. 1862
    c. 1863
    d. 1864

201. Who was Union General Ulysses S. Grant's primary opponent during the campaign?
    a. Robert E. Lee
    b. William Tecumseh Sherman
    c. Braxton Bragg
    d. Nathan Bedford Forrest

202. **What was the overall goal of this campaign for both sides?**

a. To gain control of Richmond/to defend Richmond
b. To disrupt Confederate supply lines
c. To gain control of major rivers and ports
d. To secure political alliances with foreign powers

203. **During what battle did Union forces suffer their greatest casualties during the Overland Campaign?**

a. Battle of Spotsylvania Courthouse
b. Battle of Cold Harbor
c. Battle of North Anna River
d. Battle of the Wilderness

204. **History records the Overland Campaign as having lasted how long?**

a. Two days
b. Four years
c. Five weeks
d. One hour and twenty-seven minutes

205. **What nickname did Union General Ulysses S. Grant acquire during this campaign?**

a. The Butcher
b. The Lion
c. Old Reliable
d. Unconditional Surrender Grant

206. **During which battle were both sides unable to gain much territory or advantage?**

a. Battle of the Wilderness
b. Battle North Anna River
c. Battle of Cold Harbor
d. Battle of Spotsylvania Court House

207. **Who led Confederate forces during the Overland Campaign?**

a. Robert E. Lee
b. Nathan Bedford Forrest
c. Braxton Bragg
d. William Tecumseh Sherman

208. How many total casualties occurred due to battles and skirmishes throughout the campaign?

   a.   10,000
   b.   20,000
   c.   30,000
   d.   85,000

209. What was the Union's goal at the beginning of this campaign?

   a.   To secure political alliances with foreign powers
   b.   To gain control of Richmond, Virginia
   c.   To disrupt Confederate supply lines
   d.   To gain control of major rivers and ports

210. Which battle marked the end of General Ulysses S. Grant's Overland Campaign in Virginia?

   a.   Battle North Anna River
   b.   Battle of the Wilderness
   c.   Battle of Cold Harbor
   d.   Battle Spotsylvania Court House

211. When did General Grant succeed in cutting the last railroad linking Richmond, Virginia, with the lower South?

   a.   December 25, 1882
   b.   April 1, 1865
   c.   February 14, 1862
   d.   May 9, 1864

212. Who led Union forces during most engagements throughout this campaign?

   a.   Robert E. Lee
   b.   William Tecumseh Sherman
   c.   Braxton Bragg
   d.   Ulysses S. Grant

213. What was the Confederate goal throughout this campaign?

   a.   To gain control of major rivers and ports
   b.   To secure political alliances with foreign powers
   c.   To disrupt Union supply lines
   d.   To defend Richmond, Virginia

214. How long did the Overland Campaign last in Virginia?

  a. Three months
  b. Six months
  c. Nine months
  d. Five weeks

215. Which battle marked General Robert E. Lee's first attempt to cut off Union forces from their supply line since crossing into Virginia?

  a. Battle of the Wilderness
  b. Battle of North Anna River
  c. Battle of Cold Harbor
  d. Battle Spotsylvania Court House

216. Who ordered Union troops to assault Confederate positions during the Battle of Cold Harbor, which resulted in thousands of casualties for both sides?

  a. William Tecumseh Sherman
  b. Braxton Bragg
  c. Nathan Bedford Forrest
  d. Ulysses S. Grant

217. What was the outcome of the campaign?

  a. Union forces gained all major towns and rivers in Virginia
  b. The Confederates managed to maintain some control over key areas
  c. Both sides suffered heavy casualties but neither made significant gains
  d. Strategic Union victory

218. How many engagements took place throughout this campaign?

  a. Three major battles and dozens of skirmishes
  b. Five
  c. Seven
  d. Nine

219. Which battle lasted for several days and resulted in numerous attacks by each side against strongly fortified positions with no decisive outcome?

  a. Battle of the Wilderness
  b. Battle of North Anna River
  c. Battle of Spotsylvania Court House
  d. Battle of Cold Harbor

Appomattox Court House Surrender and End of Conflict

Gather around now for a fascinating look back at the end of America's most catastrophic conflict. The Appomattox Court House surrender put an official—and merciful—end to the American Civil War and its attendant tragedies. You may remember some facts about this momentous occasion, but we'll be asking more probing questions: What date did General Robert E. Lee surrender? Who wrote his letter of resignation? And what were the terms laid out in Lee's peace agreement with Ulysses S. Grant? Let's find all these answers and immerse ourselves further into this chapter on the Appomattox Court House surrender and end of the conflict.

220. **What date did the Confederate army's surrender at Appomattox Court House take place?**
    a. April 10, 1865
    b. April 9, 1865
    c. April 11, 1865
    d. April 12, 1865

221. **Who was in command of the Union forces during this event?**
    a. Ulysses S. Grant
    b. Edwin M. Stanton
    c. Henry W. Halleck
    d. Robert E. Lee

222. How many officers accompanied General Lee as part of his surrender party?

    a. One
    b. Six
    c. Four
    d. Three

223. During the surrender at Appomattox, what kind of uniform did General Robert E. Lee wear?

    a. Brand-new uniform complete with a sash and even a jewel-studded sword
    b. Potato sacks stitched into clothing because the South had run out of cloth
    c. Dressed in a suit and top hat, strikingly similar to what Abraham Lincoln wore
    d. Shirt, shorts, and sandals, as if he were going to the beach

224. Where was General Robert E. Lee going when he received word that President Davis and his cabinet had evacuated from Richmond on April 2?

    a. Petersburg
    b. Lynchburg
    c. Appomattox Court House
    d. Richmond

225. What document was signed by General Robert E. Lee and Ulysses S. Grant to signify the surrender of Confederate forces?

    a. A peace treaty
    b. A surrender agreement
    c. An armistice
    d. A ceasefire agreement

226. Which Confederate commander fielded an army for six full weeks after the surrender at Appomattox?

    a. Jefferson Davis
    b. E. Kirby Smith
    c. Stonewall Jackson
    d. John Breckinridge

227. What battle marked the beginning of Union Major-General Philip Sheridan's successful campaign in Virginia, which ultimately resulted in the Confederate retreat to Appomattox?

a. Battle of Five Forks
b. Battle of Cold Harbor
c. Battle of Spotsylvania Courthouse
d. Battle of Chancellorsville

228. Which state was home to Appomattox Court House at this time?

a. North Carolina
b. Virginia
c. South Carolina
d. Maryland

229. How many men, in total, were surrendered by General Lee?

a. 10,000
b. 28,000
c. 40,000
d. 70,000

230. Who was the Confederate secretary of war at the time of the Appomattox Court House surrender?

a. James Seddon
b. John C. Breckinridge
c. Judah P. Benjamin
d. William T. Sherman

231. What date did Confederate General Joseph E. Johnston formally surrender to Union forces, ending all major hostilities in North and South Carolina, Georgia, and Florida?

a. April 26, 1865
b. April 6, 1865
c. May 4, 1865
d. April 12, 1865

232. What ceremony marked the formal end of military operations during this conflict?

a. The inauguration of President Lincoln
b. The Grand Review of the Armies
c. The treaty at Fort Sumter
d. The surrender ceremony at Appomattox

233. Approximately how many Confederate prisoners of war were released following the surrender at Appomattox?

    a. 10,000
    b. 15,000
    c. 20,000
    d. 28,000

234. What type of weapon did General Robert E. Lee carry with him during this event?

    a. A sword
    b. A rifle
    c. A pistol
    d. An artillery piece

235. Who captured the Confederate supply train that delivered provisions and supplies for the hungry Confederates soon after their surrender?

    a. William T. Sherman
    b. George Meade
    c. Philip Sheridan
    d. Ulysses S. Grant

236. On what date did President Lincoln issue his Proclamation of Amnesty and Reconstruction?

    a. April 13, 1865
    b. April 14, 1865
    c. December 8, 1863
    d. April 16, 1865

237. After surrendering, Robert E. Lee later served as the president of what college?

    a. Harvard
    b. Yale
    c. Washington College
    d. Brigham Young University

238. How many days did the negotiations for the surrender at Appomattox Court House last?

    a. Two   c. Six
    b. Four   d. Eight

239. **What were some of the terms laid out in General Robert E. Lee's peace agreement with Ulysses S. Grant?**

    a. No further prosecution of Confederate officers, all Southern soldiers to return home and not take up arms again

    b. All supplies and weapons surrendered by Confederates were to be given back

    c. The Union Army would provide food and clothing until the Confederates' homes could be reached

    d. Union forces would respect private property belonging to former Confederate states

Rise of the Ku Klux Klan and Militia Groups

The period in American history following the Civil War, referred to as Reconstruction, brought profound changes and violence across the South. During this time, the Ku Klux Klan organization, along with other violent domestic terrorist organizations, used fear tactics against African American citizens seeking their basic human rights. This chapter explores both the beginnings of these various military organizations and the sects within them. Who led the Ku Klux Klan, and what were their strategies for achieving a particular goal? These are just some of the questions this chapter from *American Civil War Trivia* will answer.

240.   In what year was the Ku Klux Klan founded?

    a. 1866
    b. 1865
    c. 1970
    d. 1950

241.   What was the main goal of militia groups during the Reconstruction era?

    a. To maintain white supremacy
    b. To promote religious beliefs
    c. To create a powerful political party
    d. To support racial equality and civil rights

242. **What was the primary purpose of the first KKK organization?**
   a. Protest Reconstruction policies
   b. Maintain white supremacy over newly freed African Americans
   c. Protect African Americans from violence
   d. Create an underground railroad

243. **Who founded the Knights of Liberty militia group during Reconstruction (1865-77)?**
   a. Moses Dickson
   b. John Brown
   c. Thomas Jefferson
   d. Jesse James

244. **Where were most Ku Klux Klan meetings held during the Reconstruction era?**
   a. Streets
   b. Courthouses
   c. Backyards
   d. Cemeteries

245. **Who did militia groups during the Reconstruction period primarily target?**
   a. Government officials
   b. Immigrants
   c. African Americans
   d. Native Americans

246. **The Ku Klux Klan's activities often took place under what name?**
   a. The Invisible Empire
   b. Brotherhood of Knights
   c. Order of Liberty
   d. White Supremacy League

247. **Who was instrumental in leading and organizing the first incarnation of the Ku Klux Klan?**
   a. Nathan Bedford Forrest
   b. John Brown
   c. Thomas Jefferson
   d. Jesse James

248. How did early members dress when participating in activities associated with the KKK organization?

a. In white robes
b. In ordinary clothing
c. In military uniforms
d. In colorful costumes

249. When were most former Confederate soldiers allowed to rejoin civilian life after the Civil War ended?

a. 1865
b. 1867
c. 1868
d. 1870

250. How did the Ku Klux Klan use intimidation during Reconstruction?

a. By lynching African Americans
b. By burning crosses
c. By intimidating Black voters
d. By boycotting stores owned by African Americans

251. What year did Congress pass the first Enforcement Act to help protect the civil rights of African Americans in response to KKK violence?

a. 1870
b. 1865
c. 1968
d. 1970

252. Who was involved with the rise of several violent militia groups, including the Knights of Liberty militia group?

a. Nathan Bedford Forrest
b. John Brown
c. Thomas Jefferson
d. None of the above

253. In what ways were early Ku Klux Klan members able to keep their identities hidden while engaging in activities associated with white supremacy?

a. By wearing disguises and masks
b. By dressing up as clowns
c. By keeping silent
d. By using aliases

254. **How did the White League use violence to oppose African American rights and civil liberties?**

a. By lynching African Americans
b. By burning crosses
c. By intimidating Black voters
d. By boycotting stores owned by African Americans

255. **What political party was Nathan Bedford Forrest a member of?**

a. Republican Party
b. Whig Party
c. Libertarian Party
d. Democratic Party

256. **Where was the KKK mostly active during the Reconstruction period?**

a. Southern states
b. Northern states
c. Midwestern states
d. Western states

257. **Where did the KKK begin?**

a. Tennessee
b. Georgia
c. Alabama
d. Mississippi

258. **What Reconstruction governor of Tennessee had his official portrait spit on by former Confederate legislators?**

a. Mark Twain
b. William G. Brownlow
c. Huey Long
d. Al Gore

259. **What did the Militia Act of 1862 allow for?**

a. The authorization to use federal troops against insurrectionists
b. The formation of state militias to protect civil rights
c. The establishment of local police forces
d. The enlistment of African Americans in the Union Army

Indian Wars in the West during the American Civil War

This chapter explores how Native tribes experienced and influenced battles during this critical period as conflict erupted among Natives on both sides of the Civil War for control of their traditional lands. The Indian Wars served as a reminder that while some Native Americans were loyal citizens who fought alongside other soldiers in battle, others engaged in raids against settlers or traded vengefully with opposing forces. We will examine specific wars such as the Apache Wars, the Nez Perce War, and the Seminole Wars, along with notable figures such as Stand Watie, Geronimo, Chief Joseph, and Black Kettle. We will also take a look at key battles such as the Sand Creek Massacre at Little Big Horn and treaties like the Fort Laramie Treaty of 1868, which took place amidst wider US-Indian relations during the American Civil War era.

260. **What was one of the most devastating Indian War battles in the West after the American Civil War?**
    a. Battle of Little Bighorn
    b. Apache Wars
    c. Nez Perce War
    d. Seminole Wars

261. Who led the Confederate Native Americans against Union forces in Indian Territory during the American Civil War?
   a. Stand Watie
   b. Black Kettle
   c. Geronimo
   d. Chief Joseph

262. Where did the 1864 Sand Creek Massacre occur?
   a. Fort Sumter
   b. Big Hole Battlefield
   c. Sand Creek, Colorado
   d. Wounded Knee, South Dakota

263. Which Native American tribe fought alongside Confederate forces?
   a. Cherokees
   b. Navajos
   c. Sioux
   d. Cherokees

264. What did Union forces do to protect Kansas from Confederate invasion during the American Civil War?
   a. Destroy crops and livestock of Native Americans
   b. Blockade access to the Mississippi River
   c. Build forts along the western border
   d. Place economic sanctions on Texas

265. What tribes provided warriors for Confederate General Albert Pike?
   a. Cherokees, Creeks, Chickasaws, Choctaws, Seminoles
   b. Iroquois, Comanche, Apache, Dakota, Navajo
   c. Apache, Cheyenne, Dakota, Comanche
   d. Dakota Comanche, Iroquois, Apache

266. What was it called when the Navajo were forced out of their traditional homelands by the US government in 1863?
   a. Sand Creek Massacre
   b. Battle at Little Bighorn
   c. The Long Walk
   d. Bear Paw Mountain Skirmish

267. Which two groups signed the Treaty of Fort Laramie in 1868, which ended conflicts between the Plains peoples and white settlers?

   a. The US government and the Sioux
   b. The US government and the Comanche
   c. The US government and the Apache
   d. Confederate forces and Native Americans

268. What was the primary cause of hostilities between Union troops, Confederate sympathizers, settlers, and traders in Indian Territory during the American Civil War?

   a. The Cherokee Nation's alliance with Union
   b. Settler encroachment on traditional tribal lands
   c. Confederate raids into Kansas
   d. The US Army's refusal to pay cash for food aid provided by tribes

269. What Union General was named after a Native American chief?

   a. William Tecumseh Sherman
   b. Stand Watie
   c. Ulysses S. Grant
   d. Stonewall Jackson

270. What did Pawnee warriors do when they encountered raiding parties of Cheyenne or Arapaho during the American Civil War?

   a. Fight alongside them against Union troops
   b. Join forces with the Union Army
   c. Break into smaller raiding parties
   d. Attempt to negotiate a peaceful solution

271. Who led the Kiowa and Comanche in their fight against the US government during the Red River War (1874-1875)?

   a. Chief Joseph
   b. Geronimo
   c. Satanta
   d. Quanah Parker

272. What was the first Native American tribal group to declare loyalty to the Confederates?

    a. Choctaw
    b. Apache
    c. Navajo
    d. Dakota

273. Why did Confederate forces under General Stand Watie launch an attack on Union troops at Cabin Creek in 1863?

    a. Disrupt Union blockade of the Mississippi River
    b. To spark an Apache uprising
    c. To disrupt Union supply lines
    d. Cherokee Nation's alliance with the Confederacy

274. Halleck Tustenuggee and Opothleyahola were pro-Union Native American leaders of what tribes?

    a. Creek and Seminole
    b. Apache and Arapaho
    c. Navaho and Comanche
    d. Dakota and Lakota

275. What was the primary goal of the 1864-1866 US Army expedition led by Colonel John M. Chivington against the Cheyenne and Arapaho?

    a. Capture Confederate forces in Indian Territory
    b. Seize gold reserves from Native American tribes
    c. Drive out Plains peoples from western Kansas
    d. Close trails used for trading with the Confederacy

276. After their defeat at the Battle of Washita, what did General Philip Sheridan order his troops to do to subdue Southern Plains peoples?

    a. Destroy their villages and crops
    b. Execute all captured warriors
    c. Enforce reservation treaties on remaining tribes
    d. Imprison tribal leaders

277. Who was the leader of the Modoc tribe during its war against the Union Army?

    a. Chief Joseph
    b. Geronimo
    c. Kintpuash
    d. Cochise

278. Which Native American tribe did not participate in any battles during the American Civil War?

    a. Cherokee
    b. Shawnee
    c. Cheyenne
    d. Seminole

279. What did Confederate-aligned tribes do to gain access to food and supplies during the American Civil War?

    a. Raid Union camps
    b. Trade with settlers
    c. Steal from other tribes
    d. Conduct raids on Union supply wagons

American Civil War Battle Strategies and Weapons Technology

Through battlefield strategies, technological innovation, and weapons of war on both sides, the South fought against superior forces but still managed to win some significant battles. The following questions delve into the battle strategies employed during the Civil War. In addition, we'll explore weapons technologies used for communication and combat that resulted in some of history's most iconic engagements, such as Gettysburg and the first Bull Run. Whether you consider yourself an expert or novice when it comes to the American Civil War, there are surely interesting facts about battle tactics and weapon technology still left to be discovered.

280. What was the first battle of the American Civil War?
  a. Battle of Bull Run
  b. Battle of Antietam
  c. First Battle of Manassas
  d. Siege of Fort Sumter

281. What weapon was used by both sides during the American Civil War?
  a. Swords
  b. Cannons
  c. Rifles
  d. Cattle prods

282. What strategy did Union General Ulysses S. Grant employ to defeat Confederate forces in Virginia in 1864?

a. Total war
b. Scorched earth
c. Guerilla warfare
d. Attrition

283. Which type of technology enabled soldiers on each side to fire more quickly and accurately than ever before during the US Civil War?

a. Machine guns
b. Submarines
c. Telegraphs
d. Breech-loading rifles

284. What tactic did Confederate forces employ against Union troops at Gettysburg, Pennsylvania in 1863?

a. Blitzkrieg
b. Pincer movement
c. Guerilla warfare
d. Pickett's Charge

285. What was the name given to Union forces who used a "scorched earth" policy during the US Civil War?

a. Sherman's March
b. The Iron Brigade
c. Jackson's Raid
d. Grant's Posse

286. What Confederate resource did Sherman most frequently target during his campaigns through Georgia and South Carolina?

a. Coastal fortifications
b. Railroad lines and transportation hubs
c. Confederate government offices
d. Naval shipyards

287. By what other name is the Battle of Gettysburg known?

a. First Bull Run
b. Second Manassas
c. Antietam
d. The High Water Mark of the Confederacy

288. What strategy did Confederate General Robert E. Lee employ at Chancellorsville, VA, in May 1863, resulting in victory for his forces despite being outnumbered?

a. Blitzkrieg
b. Attrition
c. Flanking
d. Picket's Charge

289. What logistical advantage helped Confederate forces hold their lines at the First Battle of Bull Run in 1861?

a. Superior weaponry
b. Timely reinforcements arriving by railroad
c. Naval artillery support
d. Foreign military assistance

290. Who was responsible for the invention and implementation of mines as weapons of warfare during the US Civil War?

a. Robert E. Lee
b. Ulysses S. Grant
c. George G. Meade
d. Matthew Maury

291. What tactic was used in Union General William Sherman's march from Atlanta, Georgia, to Savannah, Georgia, in 1864, which destroyed everything in his path?

a. Scorched earth policy
b. Total war strategy
c. Guerilla tactics
d. Pickett's Charge

292. What type of communication technology was used between military leaders on both sides, enabling them to coordinate their strategies more effectively than ever before during the US Civil War?

a. Telegraphs
b. Machine guns
c. Submarines
d. Breech-loading rifles

293. What strategy did Confederate General Thomas "Stonewall" Jackson employ against Union forces at Chancellorsville, Virginia, in 1863, which resulted in a victory for his side?

   a. Flanking
   b. Pincer movement
   c. Guerilla warfare
   d. Pickett's Charge

294. What was the *H.L. Hunley*?

   a. A Confederate fully automated robotic soldier
   b. A Union airship
   c. A Confederate submarine
   d. A Union cryptographic cypher machine

295. Which concept best describes the Union's use of widespread destruction of infrastructure to undermine the Confederacy's ability to wage war?

   a. Attrition
   b. Limited warfare
   c. Total war
   d. Defensive warfare

296. Which type of technology enabled soldiers on each side to move more quickly and effectively than ever before during the US Civil War?

   a. Steam locomotives
   b. Submarines
   c. Telegraphs
   d. Machine guns

297. Who was responsible for the invention and implementation of torpedoes as weapons of war during the US Civil War?

   a. Robert E. Lee
   b. Ulysses S. Grant
   c. George G. Meade
   d. Matthew Maury

298. **What strategy did General William Tecumseh Sherman employ to take control of Georgia during his infamous "March to the Sea" campaign?**
   a. Blocking supply lines
   b. Burning farms and villages
   c. Starving enemy soldiers
   d. All the above

299. **What technological innovation enabled Union soldiers to fire more accurately at their enemies than ever before?**
   a. Sharpshooter training
   b. Minié balls
   c. Improved weapon design
   d. Quick-firing artillery

Medical Practices during the American Civil War

The casualties of war are often measured in terms of combat, but during the American Civil War, there was another equally devastating factor to consider: medical treatment. During a time when diseases such as dysentery and cholera ran rampant, doctors needed to think on their feet and draw from long-forgotten knowledge to care for their patients. In this chapter, we will explore questions about some of the unusual medical practices used during this period: What common illnesses plague soldiers at war? How did surgeons treat broken bones? What alternative treatments were available before surgery or amputations became necessary? And how did they maintain cleanliness and prevent infection with so few supplies available? Discover both the successes and failures in medical practices during the American Civil War.

300. What was the most common disease among Civil War soldiers?

    a. Typhus
    b. Dysentery
    c. Smallpox
    d. Cholera

301. How many amputations were performed during the American Civil War?

    a. 10,000
    b. 100,000
    c. 500,000
    d. 60,000

302. How did doctors treat wounds on the battlefields earlier in the war?
   a. Bleeding and cauterizing
   b. Surgery without anesthesia
   c. Cleaning with whiskey
   d. Bandaging only

303. What type of surgical procedure was used by surgeons during the war as an alternative to amputation when possible?
   a. Skin grafting
   b. Internal fixation
   c. Bone transplantation
   d. External fixation

304. What was the most common type of anesthesia used during Civil War medical practices?
   a. Ether
   b. Cocaine
   c. Morphine
   d. Nitrous oxide

305. How did Civil War doctors try to prevent infection?
   a. Bleeding and cauterizing
   b. By covering wounds with honey
   c. By applying maggots to infected areas
   d. By using alcohol on bandages

306. Where did wounded soldiers receive their initial care in the field?
   a. In ambulance wagons
   b. In makeshift hospitals
   c. On battlefields
   d. At local farms

307. What was one way surgeons tried to reduce pain during an amputation procedure?
   a. Applying chloroform
   b. Administering opium
   c. Slicing through the skin quickly
   d. Rubbing ice onto the wound site

308. Which of these techniques were not used to treat infections caused by gunshot or knife wounds?

   a. Antibiotic creams and penicillin injections
   b. Bleeding
   c. Maggot therapy
   d. Cauterization

309. What was one of the primary ways to ensure that medical practices during the Civil War were effective?

   a. Limited access to antibiotics
   b. Strict sanitation protocols
   c. Exhaustive clinical trials
   d. Established protocols for care and treatment

310. What type of medicine was used to treat illnesses such as malaria and dysentery during the war?

   a. Quinine
   b. Chloroform
   c. Morphine
   d. Ether

311. Who served as nurses on battlefields during the American Civil War?

   a. Men only
   b. Women only
   c. Men and women
   d. Doctors only

312. How did surgeons treat broken bones during the Civil War?

   a. By setting them in plaster casts
   b. With bone grafts
   c. Through amputation
   d. By using splints and traction

313. How were medical supplies typically transported from one location to another during the Civil War?

   a. On horseback
   b. In oxen-driven carts
   c. By boat
   d. On foot

314. **How did surgeons reduce inflammation caused by wounds and infections?**
   a. By using leeches
   b. With cold compresses
   c. With mustard plasters
   d. All of the above

315. **Where were wounded soldiers typically sent for treatment after they received initial care in the field?**
   a. Local farms
   b. Military hospitals
   c. Hotels
   d. Churches

316. **Who was considered one of the most innovative surgeons during the Civil War?**
   a. Dr. William Hammond
   b. Dr. Jonathan Letterman
   c. Dr. Joseph Lister
   d. Dr. John Bell

317. **How did doctors disinfect instruments and other medical supplies during the Civil War?**
   a. By boiling them
   b. With lye
   c. By burying them
   d. They did not disinfect them

318. **What percentage of the soldiers in the Civil War died due to disease?**
   a. 15 percent
   b. 25 percent
   c. 30 percent
   d. 60 percent

319. **What factor made it difficult for medical staff to treat the wounded during the Civil War?**
   a. Inadequate supplies and resources
   b. Lack of modern equipment
   c. Unsanitary conditions
   d. Insufficient personnel

Railroads and Blockades during the American Civil War

From transporting troops and supplies to connecting ports to inland areas, railroads played a critical role in aiding Confederate forces during the American Civil War. But Union blockade fleets deployed at sea worked just as hard to cut off access to weapons shipments, food and medical supplies, and clothes for soldiers in Confederacy-held territories. In this chapter on railroads and blockades during the American Civil War, you will find questions about how leaders from both sides used these transportation networks strategically, as well as how their efforts ultimately affected military operations involved in key battles between the North and South. Plus, explore interesting facts ranging from strategies like false flag vessels employing deceptive tactics to the larger impacts on civilian life across Southern states. Are you ready for some Civil War trivia?

320. **What role did the railroads play in aiding Confederate forces during the American Civil War?**
    a. Transporting troops and supplies
    b. Connecting ports to inland areas
    c. Smuggling contraband products
    d. All the above

321. **The Union blockade was intended to prevent which of the following from reaching Confederacy-held territories?**
   a. Weapons shipments
   b. Food and medical supplies
   c. Clothes for soldiers
   d. All the above

322. **What impact did the Union blockade have on Confederate military operations?**
   a. It weakened their ability to fight by cutting off supplies
   b. It increased morale among Confederate soldiers
   c. It made it easier for troops to travel between battlefields
   d. None—the blockade did not affect Confederate forces

323. **What was one strategy used by Confederate-held ports to evade Union blockades?**
   a. Establishing false flag vessels to disguise ships as neutral traders
   b. Using secret passageways and tunnels leading from landlocked areas out into open water
   c. Hiding behind natural barriers like islands or sandbars
   d. Deploying submarines with superior stealth capabilities

324. **How were railroads used by both sides during the American Civil War?**
   a. Transporting weapons and ammunition for battlefronts
   b. Supplying food rations and medical care for wounded soldiers
   c. Connecting ports to inland areas for strategic movement of troops
   d. All the above

325. **Why did some Southern states push for increased railroad construction during the American Civil War?**
   a. To support military operations
   b. To increase trade and economic activity
   c. To provide an escape route for Confederate troops
   d. All the above

326. **What was a major advantage that Union forces had over their Confederate counterparts regarding railroads and blockades during the American Civil War?**

   a. More extensive railroad networks throughout Northern states

   b. Access to more advanced transportation technologies

   c. Greater financial resources to invest in infrastructure

   d. More experienced ship captains leading blockade fleets

327. **How did the Union blockade affect civilian life in Confederate-held territories?**

   a. It caused extreme shortages of food and medical supplies

   b. It hindered trade between states, leading to economic hardship

   c. It led to a rise in crime rates due to desperation

   d. All the above

328. **Which of the following railroad networks were used by Confederacy forces during the American Civil War?**

   a. The Southern Railroad Network

   b. The Northern Railway System

   c. The Transcontinental Railway Line

   d. The East and West Coast Railways

329. **What kind of impact did the Union blockade have on the Confederate economy?**

   a. It weakened their currency by cutting off trade with other countries

   b. It caused common goods to become scarce and expensive

   c. It led to an increase in tax rates for citizens

   d. All the above

330. **Why was it difficult for Union forces to maintain the blockade of Confederate-held ports?**

   a. Confederacy forces had superior naval vessels

   b. Confederacy ships used secret passageways and tunnels to evade blockades

   c. Union fleets were unable to match the speed of some Confederate ships

   d. All the above

331. Why did some Northern states such as Pennsylvania increase
their railway construction efforts during the American Civil War?

  a. To provide an escape route for Confederate troops
  b. To establish trade routes with Confederacy-held territories
  c. To support military operations in the battlefronts
  d. To strengthen their economy by creating new jobs

332. What kind of impact did the Union blockade have on
international relations?

  a. It increased tensions between European countries and the
US
  b. It damaged diplomatic ties between US and Confederacy
forces
  c. It made it more difficult for Union ships to travel through
foreign waters
  d. All the above

333. How did the Union blockade affect the international trade of
Confederacy-held territories?

  a. It weakened their currency by cutting off access to foreign
markets
  b. It caused common goods to become scarce and expensive
  c. It hindered diplomatic relations between the US and other
countries
  d. All the above

334. Which Union general proposed to use railroads as an offensive
weapon against Confederate forces in 1862?

  a. William Tecumseh Sherman
  b. Ambrose Burnside
  c. Ulysses S. Grant
  d. Ormsby M. Mitchel

335. How many miles were included in the Federal Railroad System
at its peak during the war?

  a. 5,000
  b. 10,000
  c. 15,000
  d. 20,000

336. Which state had hundreds of miles of railroad track destroyed during the Civil War?

   a. Texas
   b. Mississippi
   c. Georgia
   d. West Virginia

337. What was one way that railroads helped win battles in the American Civil War?

   a. Moving supplies quickly to where they were needed
   b. Transporting large numbers of soldiers
   c. Disrupting supply lines
   d. All the above

338. Which event marked the first major Union effort to disrupt Confederate railroad operations?

   a. The Great Locomotive Chase of 1862
   b. Union blockade of Confederate ports in 1861
   c. Richmond-Petersburg Campaign of 1864
   d. Siege of Vicksburg in 1863

339. How did Confederate forces block railroads from being used by Union troops?

   a. Burned bridges
   b. Seized engines
   c. Cut rails
   d. All the above

Diplomatic Relations during the American Civil War

The American Civil War brought about major changes in the diplomatic relations between the United States and other nations around the world. In this chapter, we will explore how external forces both hindered and helped during key moments of conflict. From Confederate representatives sent abroad to gain foreign recognition of their independence to Union efforts to raise legitimacy for their cause, questions surrounding international diplomacy have always been integral parts of Civil War history. Discovering these answers can help us better understand why different nations chose sides as well as what interests were at stake for each country involved in these disputes. In this chapter full of interesting facts and fascinating stories, you'll learn more about diplomatic relations during one of America's most defining moments in history.

340. What was the first major diplomatic incident of the Civil War?
    a. The Trent Affair
    b. The Emancipation Proclamation
    c. Confederate victory at Bull Run
    d. Lincoln's call for volunteers

341. **Who became a diplomat representing the Confederacy in Europe?**

  a. William Seward
  b. James M. Mason
  c. Ulysses S. Grant
  d. Robert E. Lee

342. **Which country recognized the Confederacy as a belligerent power?**

  a. France
  b. Japan
  c. Russia
  d. Mexico

343. **How did Jefferson Davis counter US government efforts to gain legitimacy abroad during the Civil War?**

  a. He refused foreign ambassadors access to his cabinet officials
  b. He accepted foreign ambassadors and negotiated treaties with them
  c. He sent representatives abroad to negotiate recognition from countries he viewed as allies
  d. All the above

344. **Which European nation offered diplomatic recognition to both North and South during the American Civil War?**

  a. None
  b. Great Britain
  c. Russia
  d. Spain

345. **What was the purpose of the diplomatic mission sent by Jefferson Davis to Europe in 1861?**

  a. To gain recognition for Confederate independence
  b. To negotiate an alliance with France and other European countries
  c. To prevent interference from foreign nations
  d. All the above

346. How did Abraham Lincoln respond when British Minister Lord Lyons requested information on the Union blockade of Confederate ports?

a. He denied him access to any confidential documents
b. He provided full details on the Union's strategy and plans
c. He refused to answer any specific questions related to military activity
d. None of the above

347. Who led the secret mission that attempted to secure recognition from Napoleon III during the American Civil War?

a. William Seward
b. James Mason
c. Judah P. Benjamin
d. Robert E. Lee

348. Why did Emperor Franz Joseph refuse diplomatic representation by the Confederacy during the American Civil War?

a. Austria had strong economic ties with Northern states
b. The emperor was a strong ally of the United States
c. Austria did not support slavery
d. None of the above

349. Who was the lead negotiator for the Confederacy during negotiations with Great Britain?

a. William Seward
b. James Mason
c. Judah P. Benjamin
d. Robert E. Lee

350. How did the US government respond to reports about diplomatic missions from Confederate agents in Europe?

a. They provided full support and resources to those efforts
b. They adopted policies designed to prevent any foreign recognition of Confederate independence
c. They actively sought out and arrested suspected sympathizers
d. None of the above

351. What caused Napoleon III's refusal to recognize the Confederacy as an independent nation during the American Civil War?

   a. French opposition to slavery
   b. Economic ties with Northern states
   c. British pressure against recognizing Southern independence
   d. Fear that it would provoke US military action against France

352. Why were many European nations reluctant to diplomatically recognize either side during the American Civil War?

   a. The threat of US retaliation
   b. Fear of involvement in a long and costly war
   c. Lack of political will to take sides
   d. All the above

353. Which factor most influenced British public opinion against recognizing the Confederacy as the war progressed?

   a. Southern cotton shortages
   b. The Emancipation Proclamation
   c. Confederate naval victories
   d. Pressure from France

354. What was the result for European nations that decided to recognize the Confederacy as "belligerent"?

   a. United States embargo against their products
   b. US military intervention in Europe
   c. Loss of access to US markets
   d. Limited trade with the Confederacy without triggering war with the Union

355. Which of the following countries allowed the Confederates to build ships in their shipyards during the American Civil War?

   a. France
   b. Japan
   c. Russia
   d. Spain

356. **What was the main reason the British refused to diplomatically recognize either side during the American Civil War?**
   a. British opposition to slavery
   b. Fear of involvement in a long and costly war
   c. Lack of political will to take sides
   d. All the above

357. **What was the main reason France refused to diplomatically recognize either side during the American Civil War?**
   a. French support for the Union cause
   b. Economic ties with Northern states
   c. Fear that it would provoke US military action against France
   d. None of the above

358. **How did Confederate agents abroad respond when Napoleon III refused diplomatic recognition for the Confederacy?**
   a. They continued their efforts to gain recognition from other countries
   b. They stopped their diplomatic activities and returned home
   c. They sought financial assistance from other European nations
   d. All the above

359. **What was a major diplomatic success achieved by the Union during the American Civil War?**
   a. Securing a formal military alliance with Britain
   b. Preventing European recognition of Confederate independence
   c. Forcing France to abandon its empire in Mexico
   d. Gaining recognition of the Confederacy as a belligerent power

Propaganda during the American Civil War

Propaganda proved to be a powerful weapon during the American Civil War. To help their cause, both Union and Confederate forces used newspapers, magazines, posters, pamphlets, and cartoons to sway public opinion in their favor. During this time of national conflict, propagandists sought to stir emotion among citizens by depicting the war through artful imagery or important messages. Through these tactics, each side promoted initiatives such as enlistment campaigns or emphasized themes such as the evils of slavery. In this chapter, we will explore some of the most significant efforts made in terms of Civil War propaganda on both sides and examine questions related to key figures involved.

360. What was the main purpose of Civil War propaganda?
    a. To rally citizens behind a cause
    b. To encourage enlistment in the army
    c. To raise money for medical supplies
    d. Both A and B

361. Which type of documents were used to spread propaganda during the American Civil War?
    a. Newspapers and magazines
    b. Posters and pamphlets
    c. Books and journals
    d. Both A and B

362. **Who is credited as one of the most prolific propagandists during the American Civil War?**

   a. Thomas Nast
   b. Abraham Lincoln
   c. John Brown
   d. Ulysses S. Grant

363. **What form did Thomas Nast's cartoons take when conveying his political messages about slavery, secession, or Union loyalty?**

   a. Comic strips
   b. Narrative poems
   c. Paintings
   d. Political posters

364. **What did many pro-Union posters depict to sway public opinion in favor of fighting for the Union?**

   a. The moral evils of slavery
   b. Images of strong soldiers
   c. Pictures of defeated battles
   d. The destruction of the Confederacy's flag

365. **How were Confederate supporters portrayed in propaganda materials produced by Northerners?**

   a. As cruel oppressors
   b. As honorable citizens
   c. As brave defenders of liberty
   d. As loyal patriots

366. **Which cartoon character became very popular with both Northern and Southern audiences during the American Civil War?**

   a. Uncle Sam
   b. John Bull
   c. Mr. Punch
   d. Falstaff

367. **Which organization distributed anti-slavery propaganda during the American Civil War?**

   a. The Abolitionists
   b. The Union
   c. The Anti-Slavery Society
   d. The Confederacy

368. **What did Confederate propagandists use to encourage enlistment in their army?**

    a. Songs and poems
    b. Drawings and paintings
    c. Posters and pamphlets
    d. Radio broadcasts

369. **How were Northern soldiers portrayed in pro-Confederate propaganda materials produced by Southerners?**

    a. As brutal oppressors
    b. As brave fighters
    c. As loyal citizens
    d. As ignorant buffoons

370. **How successful was the Peace Democrats anti-draft campaign?**

    a. It achieved great success
    b. It had mixed outcomes
    c. It failed
    d. It had a significant impact but ultimately failed to achieve its main goal

371. **What message did many posters try to convey about joining the Union Army?**

    a. It would bring glory and honor
    b. It would be a fun adventure
    c. It offered great financial rewards
    d. Both A and C

372. **What did many Confederate posters depict to rally people behind their cause?**

    a. Slavery as a moral evil
    b. Images of defeated battles
    c. The Confederacy's flag being destroyed
    d. Pictures of strong soldiers

373. **What was an unfavorable nickname of General Ulysses S. Grant?**

    a. Unconditional Surrender Grant
    b. The Beast
    c. General Halfway
    d. The Butcher

374. **How did Confederate propaganda try to rally public opinion in favor of their cause?**
   a. By appealing to people's patriotic sentiments
   b. By depicting slavery as a moral evil
   c. By portraying the Union as a threat to democracy
   d. By encouraging enlistment in their army

375. **Which event is not associated with Confederate propaganda efforts during the war?**
   a. Establishing military tribunals
   b. Burning Atlanta
   c. Demonizing African American troops
   d. Publishing articles about Lincoln's policies

376. **Who wrote The Battle Cry of Freedom: The Civil War Era?**
   a. James McPherson
   b. William Sherman
   c. Abraham Lincoln
   d. George McClellan

377. **How did Union propagandists try to portray Abraham Lincoln during the war?**
   a. As a wise leader who guided the nation through difficult times
   b. As an incompetent politician who made too many mistakes
   c. As someone with no real power over soldiers or politicians
   d. As an evil dictator who oppressed his people

378. **Who wrote *The Impending Crisis of the South,* one of the most influential pieces of Southern wartime propaganda?**
   a. Hinton Rowan Helper
   b. William Sherman
   c. George McClellan
   d. Abraham Lincoln

379. **How did Confederate propagandists try to portray Robert E. Lee during the war?**
   a. As a wise leader whose strategy won key victories for the South
   b. As an incompetent general who made too many mistakes
   c. As an evil dictator who oppressed his own people
   d. As someone with no real power over soldiers or politicians

Use of Photography as a Tool to Document the American Civil War

The American Civil War was a bloody conflict that not only shaped the future of America but also revolutionized photography. Through the use of photos, soldiers were suddenly immortalized in time, and war's devastating effects became more visible to those on both sides of the battlefield. Nowhere is this truth seen better than through a famous photographer who would become known as the "Father of Photojournalism" for his stirring pictures documenting life during the Civil War. Not only did he take field photographs at key battles, but he also employed commercial photographers to supplement his work with images from other areas around the country. But it wasn't just one man who left an indelible mark by capturing iconic moments using a variety of techniques. Read on to discover the use of photography as it evolved and immortalized this crucial event in United States history.

380. **Who was the first American photographer to take pictures in battle?**
    a. Alexander Gardner
    b. Mathew Brady
    c. Timothy O'Sullivan
    d. James Gibson

381. What did this photographer do to document the war?
    a. Kept a diary of his experiences as a soldier in the war
    b. Wrote letters and articles describing battles
    c. Photographed battlefields and portraits of generals
    d. Took paintings showing key events during the war

382. Which group was primarily responsible for taking photographs on behalf of both sides during the Civil War?
    a. Union photographers
    b. Confederate photographers
    c. Private contractors
    d. Soldiers with personal cameras

383. What type of equipment did this first photographer use to take photographs during the Civil War?
    a. Daguerreotype camera
    b. Digital SLR camera
    c. Polaroid instant camera
    d. Box-shaped wet-plate camera

384. What did the first Civil War photographer's photographs help to do?
    a. Record battles and landscapes
    b. Show the effects of war on civilians
    c. Tell stories about soldiers' daily lives
    d. All the above

385. What type of technology allowed photographers to produce multiple copies from one negative during the Civil War?
    a. Instant photography
    b. Wet plate collodion process
    c. Digital printing
    d. Lithography

386. In what year did photographic coverage become popular during the Civil War?
    a. 1859
    b. 1861
    c. 1863
    d. 1865

387. How were the first photographer's pictures used by newspapers and magazines during the Civil War?

   a. As illustrations for articles written at that time
   b. To create propaganda posters
   c. As covers for books published after the war had ended
   d. Both a and b

388. What was the purpose of photographing dead soldiers during the Civil War?

   a. To capture images of heroes for posterity
   b. To honor and remember those who had died
   c. As evidence to prove their deaths
   d. All the above

389. What was used to determine which photographs would be printed in newspapers and magazines during the American Civil War?

   a. How much detail could be seen in them
   b. Their artistic value
   c. Their relevance to current events
   d. The photographer's reputation

390. Who took some of the most iconic photographs from battles such as Antietam, Gettysburg, Chattanooga, etc.?

   a. Timothy O'Sullivan
   b. Alexander Gardner
   c. James Gibson
   d. All the above

391. How did photographers travel with their equipment while documenting battlefields during the American Civil War?

   a. In horse-drawn carriages or wagons
   b. On foot carrying their equipment on pack horses
   c. By train with special freight cars equipped for transporting photographic materials
   d. All the above

392. **What was the main challenge for photographers during the Civil War?**
   a. Obtaining access to battle sites
   b. Keeping their equipment safe
   c. Navigating terrain while carrying heavy photographic gear
   d. All the above

393. **What type of plates were used in the wet plate collodion process, which became popular during the American Civil War?**
   a. Copper sheets coated with nitrate emulsion
   b. Glass sheets coated with silver halide crystals
   c. Iron-coated glass plates
   d. Plastic films embedded with silver ions

394. **What did photographers do to protect their plates from the elements while traveling with them?**
   a. Kept them in tightly sealed boxes
   b. Carried umbrellas
   c. Wear protective clothing and hats
   d. All the above

395. **How did Mathew Brady fund his projects during the Civil War?**
   a. He sold his photographs to newspapers and magazines for publication
   b. He received grants from the government
   c. He raised money from private donors
   d. All the above

396. **Which photographer took some of the earliest known battlefield photos at Antietam Creek, Maryland in 1862?**
   a. Timothy O'Sullivan
   b. Alexander Gardner
   c. James Gibson
   d. Mathew Brady

397. **What type of lenses were typically used by photographers during the American Civil War?**
   a. Petzval portrait lenses
   b. Wide-angle lenses
   c. Telephoto lenses
   d. Fisheye lenses

398.   Which of these photographers is best known for documenting the aftermath of Gettysburg?

    a.   Mathew Brady
    b.   Timothy O'Sullivan
    c.   Alexander Gardner
    d.   James Gibson

399.   Where did this first photographer set up his studio during the American Civil War?

    a.   Washington, D.C.
    b.   Richmond, Virginia
    c.   New York City
    d.   Boston, Massachusetts

African Americans during the Civil War

Discover the role of African Americans during the American Civil War—their sacrifices, struggles, and triumphs—with this captivating chapter of *American Civil War Trivia*. Learn more about how many fought for the Union, what rights they were granted after slavery was abolished, and who became America's first Black general. Test your knowledge on topics such as legislation granting citizenship to former slaves and ratified amendments that provided equal protection under federal law. With questions ranging from which Confederate general didn't support arming Black troops to where freedmen fled in search of better economic opportunities, you'll be sure to gain insight into one of the most tumultuous times in US history.

400. How many African Americans fought for the Union during the Civil War?

    a. 10,000

    b. 50,000

    c. 150,000

    d. 200,000

401. What US state was the first to allow African Americans to vote?

    a. Massachusetts

    b. New York

    c. Michigan

    d. Ohio

402. How many African American soldiers received the Medal of Honor for their service during the Civil War?

   a. Five
   b. Twenty-five
   c. Fifty
   d. One hundred

403. After slavery was abolished, what did former slaves do with newly found freedom?

   a. Enlist in the armed forces
   b. Journeyed north
   c. Became farmers
   d. All the above

404. What legislation provided citizenship rights and equal protection under federal law for African Americans after the Civil War?

   a. The Fourteenth Amendment
   b. The Fifteenth Amendment
   c. The Thirteenth Amendment
   d. The Sixteenth Amendment

405. Which Confederate general initially opposed arming African American troops?

   a. Stonewall Jackson
   b. Robert E. Lee
   c. Joseph Johnston
   d. Braxton Bragg

406. What was the name of the first African American regiment formed after the Emancipation Proclamation?

   a. The Massachusetts 54th
   b. The Louisiana Native Guards
   c. The Ohio 9th
   d. The New York 6th Infantry Regiment

407. How many African American soldiers died during the Civil War?

   a. 5,000
   b. 10,000
   c. 20,000
   d. 30,000

408. Approximately what percentage of all African Americans alive at that time served in some capacity as a soldier or sailor for either side during the Civil War?

    a. 2 percent
    b. 5 percent
    c. 10 percent
    d. 12 percent

409. Where and when was the first major engagement of the war in which African American troops actively participated for the Union?

    a. Port Hudson, Louisiana on May 27, 1863
    b. Orlando, Florida, October 1, 1862
    c. Providence, Rhode Island, December 22, 1864
    d. Dallas, Texas, January 12, 1963

410. What was the name of the largest and most successful African American regiment in the Union Army?

    a. The Massachusetts 54th
    b. The Louisiana Native Guards
    c. The Ohio 9th
    d. The New York 6th Infantry Regiment

411. Where did freedmen flee during Reconstruction for better economic opportunities and civil rights protections?

    a. North Carolina
    b. South Carolina
    c. Mississippi
    d. Kansas

412. How many African Americans enlisted into state militias between 1861 and 1865, according to data from eleven states with reliable records?

    a. 150,000
    b. 200,000
    c. 250,000
    d. 180,000

413. When were African Americans allowed to receive pensions from their service during wartime as veterans recognized by Congress?

a. 1890s
b. 1880s
c. 1910s
d. 1920s

414. Who was the first African American to receive a Congressional Medal of Honor?

a. John Jordan
b. William Carney
c. Henry Johnson
d. Frederick Douglass

415. Who was the first government official to openly call for the enlistment of African American troops during the Civil War?

a. Democrat Vice President Andrew Johnson
b. Republican Secretary of War Simon Cameron
c. Libertarian Congressman Justin Amash
d. Whig Senator Henry Clay

416. In 1860, Washington, D.C., had a population of around 75, Of this population, how many were African American?

a. Close to 30,000
b. Over 50,000
c. Approximately 15,000
d. None

417. Who was the first African American to become a general in the United States Army?

a. Benjamin O. Davis
b. Jeremiah Simpkins
c. John Conyers
d. William Hays

418. Where and when did Confederate soldiers allegedly run over a group of African American troops with wagons?

a. Poison Springs, Arkansas, April 18, 1864
b. Chicago, Illinois, December 23, 1865
c. New Orleans, Louisiana, March 3, 1862
d. Gettysburg, Pennsylvania, May 9, 1863

419. **What did the Union Army do to protect African-American families during Reconstruction?**
   a. Set up segregated schools
   b. Established the Freedmen's Bureau
   c. Created refugee camps
   d. Enforced Jim Crow laws

Women on Both Sides of the American Civil War: Nurses, Spies, and Soldiers

During the American Civil War, women played a critical role on both sides of the conflict. From nurses to spies and from soldiers in disguise to advocates for African-American emancipation, the contributions of these brave women helped shape history. In this chapter, we'll explore trivia questions about remarkable individuals like Clara Barton, Harriet Tubman, Rose O'Neal Greenhow, and more who made their mark during the war that waged between North and South. Let's see if you can answer questions like these: What was the name of the first female combat soldier in American history during this war? How many spies from the Union and the Confederacy were present? Test your knowledge right now.

420. What was the name of a female army surgeon for the Union who became a POW during the Civil War?

    a. Mary Edwards Walker
    b. Harriet Tubman
    c. Clara Barton
    d. Rose O'Neal Greenhow

421. How many women served as Union and Confederate spies during the Civil War?

    a. Hundreds, though the exact number is unknown
    b. 100-150
    c. 50-100
    d. 25-50

422. Who wrote a book about her experiences as a Confederate spy?

    a. Belle Boyd
    b. Loreta Velazquez
    c. Rose O'Neal Greenhow
    d. All the above

423. Which of these professions did Clara Barton not have before working as an army nurse during the US Civil War?

    a. Teacher
    b. Nurse
    c. Humanitarian
    d. Tailor

424. Who was the Civil War nurse, nicknamed "Dragon" by her colleagues, who worked as the Union's superintendent of female nurses during the war?

    a. Florence Nightingale
    b. Queen Victoria
    c. Katy Perry
    d. Dorothea Lynde Dix

425. Which Union nurse is credited with creating the first battlefield ambulance corps during the Civil War?

    a. Clara Barton
    b. Dorothea Dix
    c. Mary Livermore
    d. Amelia Bloomer

426. What was Harriet Tubman's role in the American Civil War?

    a. Nurse
    b. Soldier
    c. Spy
    d. All the above

427. How did Loreta Janeta Velazquez disguise herself to fight for the Confederacy as Harry T. Buford?

    a. As an Irish soldier
    b. As a male slave
    c. As an African American soldier
    d. As a white male soldier

428. Who established a military hospital for Confederate soldiers in Richmond, Virginia, during the Civil War?

    a. Annie Wittenmyer
    b. Sally Louisa Tompkins
    c. Mary Edwards Walker
    d. Rose O'Neal Greenhow

429. What was Harriet Tubman most famous for during the Civil War?

    a. Nursing
    b. Spying
    c. Leading troops in battle
    d. Both B and C

430. In what Southern city, on April 2, 1863, did a group of women instigate a "Bread Riot" over wartime food shortages?

    a. New Orleans, Louisiana
    b. Richmond, Virginia
    c. Nashville, Tennessee
    d. Louisville, Kentucky

431. How many African American nurses served in the Union Army during the US Civil War?

    a. Over 500
    b. Over 100
    c. Less than 50
    d. None

432. Nurses working with which branch of the military saw one of their own become known as "The Angel of the Battlefield"?

    a. Navy
    b. Marines
    c. Air Force
    d. Army

433. Which female nurse is most often credited with introducing and promoting hospital tenting in Union military medical care during the Civil War?

a. Clara Barton
b. Annie Wittenmyer
c. Mary Ann Bickerdyke
d. Dorothea Dix

434. What year did Florence Nightingale become the first woman to receive the Royal Red Cross from Queen Victoria—serving as an inspiration for nurses during the American Civil War?

a. 1854
b. 1861
c. 1865
d. 1883

435. Who was known as "The Confederate Joan of Arc" for her bravery during battle and skillful rallying of troops?

a. Emma Edmonds
b. Rose O'Neal Greenhow
c. Loreta Janeta Velazquez
d. Annie Wittenmyer

436. How many women disguised themselves as men to fight on behalf of both sides in the Civil War?

a. About 500
b. About 250
c. Less than 100
d. Up to 1,000

437. What were so-called "respectable women" who traveled with the army to serve in various assisting roles known as?

a. Good girls
b. Abe's angels
c. Vivandieres
d. Valkyries

438. What was the name of the first African American army nurse of the Civil War?

    a. Susie King Taylor

    b. Annie Wittenmyer

    c. Harriet Tubman

    d. Loreta Janeta Velazquez

439. Which female nurse was the first woman awarded the Medal of Honor?

    a. Mary Edwards Walker

    b. Annie Wittenmyer

    c. Clara Barton

    d. Dorothea Dix

Reconstruction Period Following War

The end of the American Civil War in 1865 marked a significant turning point for America and its citizens. While the war had ended with the Confederate surrender, rebuilding was now left to Congress. In this chapter, we take a closer look at the Reconstruction period that followed, exploring these and other questions: How long did it last? What were some of its main goals? How did African Americans gain access to education during these turbulent years? And ultimately, what mark did this era leave on our nation's history? Ready your thinking caps—it's time to test your knowledge on all things surrounding Reconstruction.

440. **What years mark the beginning and end of the Reconstruction period following the Civil War?**
    a. 1861-1865
    b. 1865-1867
    c. 1865-1877
    d. 1877-1900

441. **What was the main goal of Reconstruction following the Civil War?**
    a. Grant former slaves full voting rights
    b. Reunite the North and South into a unified country
    c. Rebuild infrastructure destroyed by war
    d. Strengthen national security

442. **What were sharecroppers?**

   a. Small farmers who owned their land
   b. Farm workers who leased land from planters
   c. Workers employed on large plantations
   d. Factory laborers in Northern cities

443. **When did Congress pass legislation to ensure equal civil rights regardless of race or color?**

   a. 1868
   b. 1870
   c. 1875
   d. All the above

444. **Which leader had an important role in Reconstruction efforts after the Civil War?**

   a. Ulysses S. Grant
   b. Abraham Lincoln
   c. Andrew Johnson
   d. Robert E. Lee

445. **What was the name of the plan that allowed former Confederate states to rejoin the Union in 1865?**

   a. The Reconstruction Plan
   b. The Wade-Davis Bill
   c. The Great Compromise
   d. The Ten Percent Plan

446. **About how many African Americans were elected to public office during this period?**

   a. Fifty
   b. One hundred
   c. One thousand
   d. Two thousand

447. **Who were the Radical Republicans?**

   a. Politicians who supported civil rights for African Americans
   b. Politicians who opposed Reconstruction efforts
   c. Former Confederate generals
   d. Pro-slavery activists

448. **How did African Americans gain access to education during Reconstruction?**
   a. By attending segregated schools run by churches and charities
   b. By attending newly-established public schools open to everyone
   c. By gaining admission into colleges created specifically for them
   d. All the above

449. **What were the Black Codes?**
   a. Laws that sought to grant African American civil rights
   b. Laws that granted full voting rights to African Americans
   c. Laws that allowed former slaves to own land
   d. None of the above

450. **Why did some Northerners oppose Reconstruction efforts in the South?**
   a. They feared it would harm Northern businesses
   b. They opposed giving political power to newly freed slaves
   c. They feared it would strengthen Southern states and give political power to newly freed slave states
   d. All the above

451. **How many amendments were added during this period as part of Reconstruction efforts?**
   a. One
   b. Three
   c. Five
   d. Seven

452. **What was one effect of Radical Republican control over Congress after 1867?**
   a. Increase in taxes for Southern citizens
   b. Expansion of voting rights to all men
   c. Increase in the power of state governments
   d. Limitation on civil rights for African Americans

453. Which African American leader played a prominent role in advocating for civil rights during Reconstruction?

  a. Frederick Douglass
  b. Booker T. Washington
  c. W. E. B. Du Bois
  d. Marcus Garvey

454. What were some opportunities available to African Americans during Reconstruction?

  a. Working as sharecroppers
  b. Owning businesses
  c. Serving as elected officials
  d. All the above

455. How did African American participation in politics during Reconstruction help to advance civil rights?

  a. It raised awareness of racial injustice
  b. It increased support for the passage of new laws
  c. It provided a platform for sharing stories and experiences
  d. All the above

456. How were African Americans able to create communities despite difficult conditions?

  a. By forming religious organizations
  b. By establishing mutual aid societies
  c. By creating social clubs and fraternities
  d. All the above

457. What was one way that white Southerners fought against Reconstruction efforts?

  a. Instigating race riots
  b. Forming paramilitary groups
  c. Organizing political campaigns in support of African American candidates
  d. Refusing to pay taxes

458. How did Congress punish states that refused to ratify the Fourteenth Amendment?

  a. With the occupation of federal troops in those states
  b. Denial of representation in Congress
  c. Removal from Union membership
  d. Imposition of economic sanctions

459. **How did the Compromise of 1877 mark the end of Reconstruction?**
    a. It permitted federal troops to leave Southern states
    b. It allowed for full voting rights regardless of race
    c. It provided pardons to former Confederate leaders
    d. It declared African Americans as citizens with equal protection under the law

Assassination of President Lincoln

The assassination of Abraham Lincoln, the sixteenth president of the United States, was a major event in American history. It happened at a time when America was still struggling to rebuild itself after the bloody Civil War that had ended months earlier. Outlined in this chapter are questions about all aspects of this dastardly act, from who assassinated Lincoln and how they went about it to where Lincoln was buried following his death. Test your knowledge and see if you can recognize some hidden trivia facts related to one of the most terrible moments in American history.

460. Who assassinated President Abraham Lincoln?

    a. John Wilkes Booth
    b. Robert E. Lee
    c. Ulysses S. Grant
    d. Jefferson Davis

461. What month in 1865 did the assassination of President Lincoln take place?

    a. April
    b. March
    c. May
    d. June

462. **Where was President Lincoln assassinated?**
   a. Ford's Theatre
   b. The White House
   c. An open field
   d. The Capitol

463. **Who was President Lincoln's vice president?**
   a. Andrew Johnson
   b. Ulysses S. Grant
   c. Robert E. Lee
   d. Jefferson Davis

464. **How many other people were injured in addition to President Lincoln during this incident?**
   a. Four
   b. Three
   c. Two
   d. One

465. **Which weapon did John Wilkes Booth use to assassinate President Lincoln?**
   a. Gun
   b. Knife
   c. Bow and Arrow
   d. Poison

466. **After assassinating President Lincoln, where did John Wilkes Booth flee first?**
   a. Maryland
   b. Ford's Theatre
   c. Washington, D.C.
   d. Richmond, VA

467. **Where was John Wilkes Booth captured following the assassination?**
   a. Garret's Farm
   b. Ford's Theatre
   c. Washington, D.C.
   d. Richmond, VA

468. **When did John Wilkes Booth die?**

   a. April 26, 1865
   b. April 14, 1865
   c. May 1, 1865
   d. July 4, 1864

469. **How many conspirators were involved in the plot to kill Abraham Lincoln and other government officials?**

   a. Four
   b. Six
   c. Eleven
   d. Eight

470. **How many of these conspirators were executed?**

   a. Three
   b. Five
   c. Six
   d. Four

471. **What was the main motive behind John Wilkes Booth's assassination of Abraham Lincoln?**

   a. Financial Gain
   b. Revenge
   c. Racism
   d. Both B and C

472. **Who wrote the play *Our American Cousin*, which was being performed at Ford's Theatre when President Lincoln was assassinated?**

   a. Tom Taylor
   b. Edwin Stanton
   c. William Shakespeare
   d. Charles Dickens

473. **When did Vice President Andrew Johnson become president?**

   a. After winning the lottery
   b. Upon winning an impeachment trial against Lincoln in 1866
   c. He was appointed by Democratic members of Congress to appease the South
   d. Upon learning of Abraham Lincoln's death

474. **Who was the first lady of President Abraham Lincoln?**
    a. Mary Todd Lincoln
    b. Martha Washington
    c. Abigail Adams
    d. Dolley Madison

475. **What did John Wilkes Booth shout before assassinating President Lincoln?**
    a. "Sic semper tyrannis!"
    b. "The South will rise again!"
    c. "Power to the people!"
    d. "Justice for all!"

476. **How long had Abraham Lincoln served as president when he was assassinated in 1865?**
    a. Four years
    b. Eight months
    c. Five months
    d. Two weeks

477. **Where was Abraham Lincoln buried after his assassination?**
    a. Arlington National Cemetery, Virginia
    b. Oak Ridge Cemetery, Illinois
    c. Mount Olivet Cemetery, Maryland
    d. National Cathedral, Washington, D.C

478. **What was Abraham Lincoln's final speech before his assassination?**
    a. Second Inaugural Address
    b. Gettysburg Address
    c. First Inaugural Address
    d. A speech about Reconstruction and reunification

479. **Who sentenced the conspirators involved in Abraham Lincoln's assassination?**
    a. Special Judge Advocate John Bingham
    b. Secretary of War Edwin Stanton
    c. A military tribunal presided over by Major General David Hunter
    d. Associate Justice David Davis

Memorialization and Commemoration of the Civil War

The American Civil War forever changed the course of history for the young United States. To honor those brave men and women who died in battle, countless memorials have been erected across the country to commemorate their service. In this chapter of American Civil War Trivia, we will explore how these fallen heroes are remembered today with questions focused on the national cemeteries, monuments, ceremonies, and reenactments created to respect the memory of soldiers on both sides. Take up the challenge.

480. What did Abraham Lincoln create to dedicate the Gettysburg battlefield in 1863?

    a. A museum
    b. A memorial park
    c. The Soldiers' National Cemetery
    d. An amphitheater

481. Which of these is an example of how people have commemorated those who fought and died in the American Civil War?

    a. Building statues
    b. Painting murals
    c. Writing books
    d. All the above

482. What is the name of the national cemetery that was established in 1864?
    a. Fort Snelling National Cemetery
    b. Arlington National Cemetery
    c. Andersonville National Historic Site
    d. Vicksburg National Military Park

483. To honor the memory of those who fought for the Union during the Civil War, which organization was founded in 1866?
    a. United Confederate Veterans
    b. Sons of Union and Confederate Veterans
    c. Grand Army of the Republic
    d. American Legion

484. What is the name of the memorial honoring African Americans who served as part of the United States Colored Troops (USCT) during the Civil War?
    a. National Museum of African American History and Culture
    b. National Mall
    c. USCT Freedom Monument
    d. African American Civil War Memorial

485. Which is a site people visit to commemorate and remember those who fought in the Civil War?
    a. Gettysburg National Military Park
    b. Manassas National Battlefield Park
    c. Antietam National Battlefield
    d. All the above

486. What is the name of a national monument located at Appomattox Court House, Virginia, that pays tribute to soldiers who served on both sides of the Civil War?
    a. United Confederate Veterans Memorial
    b. Soldiers' and Sailors' Monument
    c. The Wall of Honor
    d. Lincoln Memorial

487. Which battle site has become one of America's most visited historical destinations since it was dedicated as a memorial park by President Abraham Lincoln in 1863?

    a. Shiloh
    b. Vicksburg
    c. Antietam
    d. Gettysburg

488. What monument was placed in 1926 at Appomattox Court House National Historic Park in Virginia?

    a. The McLean House
    b. Federal Artillery Battery Marker
    c. The Appomattox Monument
    d. North Carolina Monument

489. Which event, which took place annually from 1931 until 1968, commemorated Civil War soldiers and their families?

    a. The Confederate Reunion
    b. The Grand Army Reunion
    c. Decoration Day
    d. The Peace Festival

490. Which organization was formed to preserve Union military monuments and gravesites after the war ended?

    a. United Confederate Veterans
    b. Sons of Union Veterans of the Civil War
    c. Grand Army of the Republic
    d. American Legion

491. At the height of membership in 1890,How many veterans were members of the Grand Army of the Republic?

    a. 505
    b. 427,981
    c. 10,023
    d. 440

492. In what year did President Andrew Johnson issue the amnesty proclamation?

    a. 1865   c. 1870
    b. 1868   d. 1871

493. Which event marks the anniversary of Robert E. Lee's surrender
at Appomattox Court House on April 9, 1865?
    a. Annual Commemoration of Surrender and Freedom Day
    b. The Grand Army Reunion
    c. Confederate Reunion
    d. The Peace Festival

494. What is the name of a national cemetery located in Arlington,
Virginia, that serves as the final resting place for over 400,000
veterans?
    a. Fort Snelling National Cemetery
    b. Arlington National Cemetery
    c. Andersonville National Historic Site
    d. Vicksburg National Military Park

495. Which organization was founded by Clara Barton after the Civil
War to identify and mark the gravesites of soldiers who died
during battle?
    a. United Confederate Veterans
    b. Sons of Union and Confederate Veterans
    c. Grand Army of the Republic
    d. The Missing Soldiers Office

496. What is the name of a memorial located in Indianapolis,
Indiana, that was dedicated to Union soldiers who died during
the Civil War?
    a. United Confederate Veterans Memorial
    b. Soldiers' & Sailors' Monument
    c. Appomattox Peace Monument
    d. Lincoln Memorial

497. In what year did the first Memorial Day take place?
    a. 1865
    b. 1868
    c. 1870
    d. 1871

498. What is the goal of a Civil War re-enactment?
    a. To learn about and commemorate those who fought in the
       Civil War
    b. To recreate military strategies used during battle
    c. To demonstrate weapons and equipment
    d. All the above

499.   What is the name of a monument in Arlington National Cemetery that pays tribute to sailors and soldiers who lost their lives during the Civil War?

    a.   Soldiers' & Sailors' Monument
    b.   USCT Freedom Monument
    c.   The Civil War Unknowns Monument
    d.   Vietnam Veterans Memorial

500.   How many Confederate veterans attended the final reunion of Confederate Veterans, which was held in 1951?

    a.   Two
    b.   Five
    c.   Ten
    d.   Three

Conclusion

Throughout this book, we have explored many aspects of the American Civil War. From causes and strategies to weapons technology and medical practices, we've gained an understanding of how complicated this conflict was.

We looked at politics both at home and abroad, as well as the experiences of African Americans and women, the Northern draft riots, the Indian Wars in the West during the war, and the post-war Reconstruction period.

We also discussed memorialization and commemoration efforts that are still ongoing today for those who fought during this critical time in our nation's history.

Whether through photography or words such as Lincoln's Gettysburg Address, we have come to appreciate how far-reaching its effects were on individuals and society alike.

In conclusion, this book has provided us with a comprehensive overview of one of America's most important events, which is sure to increase our appreciation for all that was sacrificed so long ago.

Thanks for reading!

Answer Key

Causes of the American Civil War

1. a. The expansion of slavery in states and territories
2. d. Kansas-Nebraska Act
3. c. Missouri Compromise
4. d. Missouri
5. c. Limit the expansion of slavery
6. b. Fugitive slave law
7. a. Increased taxes on goods imported by Southern states from Europe
8. c. Cotton
9. a. Abraham Lincoln's election as president
10. a. All runaway slaves be returned to their owners
11. b. Stephen Douglas
12. b. The US should purchase Cuba from Spain
13. a. Election of Abraham Lincoln
14. a. Northeastern states
15. a. South Carolina
16. a. Expansion of slavery into western territories
17. c. It ruled that African Americans were not citizens and that the courts could not recognize cases filed by them at the federal level
18. b. The pro-slavery constitution of the Lecompton legislature was enforced
19. d. The Mexican-American War
20. b. Abraham Lincoln's inaugural address

US Presidential Election of 1860

21. c. Republican
22. b. Vice president of the United States
23. b. 180
24. d. John C. Breckenridge, John Bell, and Stephen A. Douglas
25. b. Slavery
26. d. 33
27. b. South Carolina
28. d. Abraham Lincoln
29. d. John Bell
30. a. James Buchanan
31. b. Increase tariffs
32. a. 152
33. d. John C. Breckenridge
34. a. Democratic
35. d. "Vote Yourself a Farm and Horses"
36. b. Telegram
37. b. California and Oregon
38. a. Other Southern states followed suit
39. b. He was against the expansion of slavery
40. b. Hannibal Hamlin

The Secession of Southern States

41. d. Eleven states
42. d. February 8, 1861
43. d. Delaware
44. a. They feared negative economic consequences
45. a. The Thirteenth Amendment
46. a. John C. Calhoun
47. a. To form their own nation based on slave labor
48. b. South Carolina
49. a. Tennessee
50. c. Six months
51. d. The Articles of Confederation
52. b. To protect themselves against foreign aggression
53. c. Christopher G. Memminger

54.   a. December 20, 1860
55.   a. To create new slave-owning territories outside US borders
56.   b. He issued an executive order
57.   d. The Union Army
58.   c. Jefferson Davis
59.   d. They ignored it
60.   b. 1861

Fort Sumter Attack and Surrender

61.   b. April 12, 1861
62.   a. General Pierre G. T. Beauregard
63.   c. Thirty-four hours
64.   a. Confederates claimed ownership of the fort and considered attempts to resupply the fort an affront to state sovereignty
65.   a. Confederate troops
66.   a. Zero
67.   c. Bombardment from Confederate artillery
68.   a. Montgomery, Alabama
69.   d. Richard Kidder Meade
70.   a. He issued a proclamation calling for 75,000 volunteers
71.   d. Major Robert Anderson
72.   c. Moderate damage
73.   a. The US Navy
74.   a. From an artillery battery located on James Island
75.   c. They were running low on food and ammunition
76.   b. Four
77.   d. He fired on the fort
78.   b. A call to arms
79.   d. The Union forces were defeated and evacuated Fort Sumter

First Battle of Bull Run/Manassas

80.   c. July 21, 1861
81.   d. P.G.T. Beauregard
82.   d. 450–700
83.   c. Virginia
84.   b. Republican Congressman Alfred Ely

85.   a. PGT Beauregard and Joseph E. Johnston
86.   a. Confederate forces had better military tactics than their counterparts
87.   d. Making an early exit to report a Union victory, only to later learn of the defeat
88.   b. Thomas J. Jackson
89.   a. Seven
90.   d. Washington, D.C.
91.   a. Confederate forces
92.   a. To seize Manassas railroad junction
93.   a. Irvin McDowell, William T. Sherman, James Longstreet
94.   c. Three days
95.   c. Irvin McDowell
96.   b. Defend territory while waiting for reinforcements
97.   c. Confederate General Bernard Bee
98.   a. Thomas J. Jackson, Bernard Bee, Joseph Johnston
99.   a. It was the first major land battle of the Civil War

Union Blockade of Confederate Ports

100.   a. To block Confederate exports and prevent supplies from entering Confederate territory
101.   d. Four
102.   d. USS Niagara
103.   b. Merchant ships
104.   a. 1861
105.   d. Wilmington, North Carolina
106.   d. They remained neutral, refusing involvement in US affairs
107.   d. All the above
108.   a. 1861
109.   c. The Anaconda Plan
110.   d. All of above
111.   c. South Carolina
112.   b. Though risky, it was profitable to get supplies into Confederate territories
113.   b. none
114.   b. By using blockade runners

115.   d. All the above
116.   b. Union capture of Fort Fisher on January 15, 1865, cut off the port
117.   a. Charleston Harbor, South Carolina
118.   a. None
119.   c. Side-wheel steamers

Battle of Antietam and Emancipation Proclamation

120.   c. The Emancipation Proclamation
121.   b. January 1,1863
122.   d. George B. McClellan
123.   b. 23,000
124.   a. Slaves within Confederate states were declared free
125.   a. 13,000 small arms and 73 cannon
126.   a. One day
127.   a. Abraham Lincoln
128.   b. Battle of Sharpsburg
129.   b. To end slavery in America
130.   d. 40,000
131.   d. It was a tactical draw that enabled the Emancipation Proclamation to be issued and enforced
132.   b. Robert E. Lee
133.   d. September 22, 1862
134.   a. Declared a Union victory
135.   d. George B. McClellan
136.   c. September 17, 1862
137.   b. It brought his army closer to Washington, D.C., providing a strategic advantage
138.   d. Telegraph wires were used to send messages between army headquarters
139.   c. To boost Confederate morale by engaging in a battle outside Confederate territory

Draft Riots in the North

140. b. 1863
141. a. Nearly a week
142. d. The poor white working-class
143. c. New York City
144. c. They suffered disproportionately
145. a. African Americans, because of their employment status
146. a. The Potato Famine
147. a. He sent Union troops
148. b. They opposed the Civil War and encouraged resistance to the draft
149. d. Native New Yorkers and recent arrivals
150. b. Partially restored
151. d. No one
152. c. Heightened racial tensions
153. c. By deploying police units
154. a. Imprisonment
155. d. None of the above
156. d. All the above
157. a. Military forces
158. c. 67
159. b. It became less favorable

Battle of Chickamauga and Battle of Nashville

160. a. General William Rosecrans
161. a. Tennessee
162. c. Union forces surrounded Confederates on Orchard Knob
163. c. 1863-1864
164. b. The Union
165. a. To surround and trap Union forces
166. a. He simply followed the sounds of battle
167. d. John Bell Hood
168. c. Two months
169. a. To draw out Union forces from Chattanooga
170. b. Braxton Bragg
171. b. The Louisville and Nashville

172.   c. Confederacy
173.   b. In the hills outside of Chattanooga
174.   a. They retreated to Alabama
175.   a. December 15, 1864
176.   c. George Thomas
177.   b. To draw out battle by attacking at multiple points
178.   d. Around 30,000
179.   d. George Thomas

Gettysburg Address Delivered by Lincoln

180.   a. 1863
181.   b. Two minutes
182.   d. Quotes from ancient literature
183.   d. Gettysburg, Pennsylvania
184.   a. Julia Ward Howe
185.   a. Pennsylvania
186.   c. Ten
187.   a. To inspire patriotism and national unity
188.   d. Abraham Lincoln
189.   a. Four score and seven years ago
190.   a. Four score and seven years ago
191.   d. All the above
192.   c. With inspiring words about freedom
193.   b. The principles of equality expressed in the Declaration of Independence
194.   d. 272
195.   The citizens attending the ceremony
196.   c. American citizens
197.   d. Soldiers' National Cemetery
198.   c. November
199.   d. Four and a half months

The Overland Campaign in Virginia

200.   d. 1864
201.   a. Robert E. Lee
202.   a. To gain control of Richmond/to defend Richmond
203.   a. Battle at Spotsylvania Courthouse
204.   c. Five weeks
205.   d. Unconditional Surrender Grant
206.   a. Battle of the Wilderness
207.   a. Robert E. Lee
208.   d. 85,000
209.   b. To defend Richmond, Virginia
210.   c. Battle of Cold Harbor
211.   b. April 1, 1865
212.   d. Ulysses S. Grant
213.   d. To gain control of Richmond, Virginia
214.   d. Five weeks
215.   a. Battle of the Wilderness
216.   d. Ulysses S. Grant
217.   d. Strategic Union victory
218.   a. Three major battles and dozens of skirmishes
219.   a. Battle at Wilderness Tavern

Appomattox Court House Surrender and End of Conflict

220.   b. April 9, 1865
221.   a. Ulysses S. Grant
222.   a. One
223.   a. Brand-new uniform complete with a sash, and even a jewel-studded sword
224.   b. Lynchburg
225.   b. A surrender agreement
226.   b. E. Kirby Smith
227.   a. Battle of Five Forks
228.   b. Virginia
229.   b. 28,000

230.   b. John C. Breckinridge
231.   a. April 26, 1865
232.   d. The surrender ceremony at Appomattox
233.   d. 28,000
234.   a. A sword
235.   c. Philip Sheridan
236.   c. December 8, 1863
237.   c. Washington College
238.   a. Two
239.   a. No further prosecution of Confederate officers, all Southern soldiers to return home and not take up arms again

Rise of the Ku Klux Klan and Militia Groups

240.   b. 1865
241.   d. To maintain white supremacy
242.   b. Maintain white supremacy over newly freed African Americans
243.   a. Moses Dickson
244.   d. Cemeteries
245.   c. African Americans
246.   a. The Invisible Empire
247.   a. Nathan Bedford Forrest
248.   d. In colorful costumes
249.   a. 1865
250.   c. By intimidating Black voters
251.   a. 1870
252.   d. None of the above
253.   a. By wearing disguises and masks
254.   b. By lynching African Americans
255.   d. Democratic Party
256.   a. Southern states
257.   a. Tennessee
258.   b. William G. Brownlow
259.   d. The enlistment of African Americans in the Union Army

Indian Wars in the West During the American Civil War

260. a. Battle of Little Bighorn
261. a. Stand Watie
262. c. Sand Creek, Colorado
263. d. Cherokees
264. c. Build forts along the western border
265. a. Cherokees, Creeks, Chickasaws, Choctaws, Seminoles
266. c. The Long Walk
267. a. The US government and the Sioux
268. b. Settler encroachment on traditional tribal lands
269. a. William Tecumseh Sherman
270. d. Attempt to negotiate a peaceful solution
271. d. Quanah Parker
272. a. Choctaw
273. c. To disrupt Union supply lines
274. a. Creek and Seminole
275. c. Drive out Plains peoples from western Kansas
276. a. Destroy their villages and crops
277. c. Kintpuash
278. c. Cheyenne
279. b. Trade with settlers

American Civil War Battle Strategies and Weapons Technology

280. d. Siege of Fort Sumter
281. c. Rifles
282. d. Attrition
283. d. Breech-loading rifles
284. d. Pickett's Charge
285. a. Sherman's March
286. b. Railroad lines and transportation hubs
287. d. The High Water Mark of the Confederacy
288. c. Flanking
289. b. Timely reinforcements arriving by railroad

290. d. Matthew Maury
291. a. Scorched earth policy
292. a. Telegraphs
293. a. Flanking
294. c. Confederate submarine
295. c. Total war
296. a. Steam locomotives
297. d. Matthew Maury
298. d. All the above
299. b. Minié Balls

Medical Practices during the American Civil War

300. b. Dysentery
301. d. 60,000
302. c. Cleaning with whiskey
303. d. External fixation
304. a. Ether
305. b. By covering wounds with honey
306. b. In makeshift hospitals
307. b. Administering opium
308. b. Penicillin injections
309. d. Established protocols for care and treatment
310. a. Quinine
311. c. Men and women
312. d. By using splints and traction
313. a. On horseback
314. d. All of the above
315. b. Military hospitals
316. b. Dr. Jonathan Letterman
317. d. They did not disinfect them
318. d. 60 percent
319. a. Inadequate supplies and resources

Railroads and Blockades during the American Civil War

320.   d. All the above
321.   d. All the above
322.   a. It weakened their ability to fight by cutting off supplies
323.   a. Establishing false flag vessels to disguise ships as neutral traders
324.   d. All the above
325.   a. To support military operations
326.   a. More extensive railroad networks throughout Northern states
327.   d. All the above
328.   a. The Southern Railroad Network
329.   d. All the above
330.   c. Union fleets were unable to match the speed of some Confederate ships
331.   c. To support military operations in the battlefronts
332.   a. It increased tensions between European countries and the US
333.   d. All the above
334.   d. George McClellan
335.   d. 20,000
336.   c. Georgia
337.   d. All the above
338.   a. The Great Locomotive Chase of 1862
339.   d. All the above

Diplomatic Relations during the American Civil War

340.   a. The Trent Affair
341.   b. James M. Mason
342.   a. France
343.   c. He sent representatives abroad to negotiate recognition from countries he viewed as allies
344.   a. None
345.   d. All the above
346.   d. None of the above
347.   b. James Mason

348. d. None of the above
349. b. James Mason
350. b. They adopted policies designed to prevent any foreign recognition of Confederate independence
351. d. Fear that it would provoke US military action against France
352. d. All the above
353. b. The Emancipation Proclamation
354. d. Limited trade with the Confederacy without triggering war with the Union
355. a. France
356. d. All the above
357. c. Fear that it would provoke US military action against France
358. a. They continued their efforts to gain recognition from other countries
359. b. Preventing European recognition of Confederate independence

Propaganda during the American Civil War

360. d. Both A and B
361. d. Both A and B
362. a. Thomas Nast
363. d. Political posters
364. a. The moral evils of slavery
365. a. As cruel oppressors
366. c. Mr. Punch
367. c. The Anti-Slavery Society
368. c. Posters and pamphlets
369. d. As brutal oppressors
370. d. It had a significant impact but ultimately failed to achieve its main goal
371. d. Both A and C
372. d. Pictures of strong soldiers
373. d. The Butcher
374. a. By appealing to people's patriotic sentiments
375. b. Burning Atlanta
376. a. James McPherson

377.   a. As a wise leader who guided the nation through difficult times
378.   a. Hinton Rowan Helper
379.   a. As a wise leader whose strategy won key victories for the South

Use of Photography as a Tool to Document the American Civil War

380.   b. Mathew Brady
381.   c. Photographed battlefields and portraits of generals
382.   c. Private contractors
383.   d. Box-shaped wet-plate camera
384.   d. All the above
385.   b. Wet plate collodion process
386.   b. 1861
387.   d. Both a and b
388.   d. All the above
389.   c. Their relevance to current events
390.   b. All the above
391.   a. In horse-drawn carriages or wagons
392.   d. All the above
393.   b. Glass sheets coated with silver halide crystals
394.   a. Kept them in tightly sealed boxes
395.   d. All the above
396.   b. Alexander Gardner
397.   a. Petzval portrait lenses
398.   b. Timothy O'Sullivan
399.   c. New York City

African Americans during the Civil War

400.   d. 200,000
401.   a. Massachusetts
402.   b. Twenty-five
403.   d. All the above
404.   a. The Fourteenth Amendment
405.   b. Robert E. Lee
406.   a. The Massachusetts 54th
407.   d. 30,000

408.   b. 5 percent
409.   a. Port Hudson, Louisiana on May 27, 1863
410.   a. The Massachusetts 54th
411.   d. Kansas
412.   d. 180,000
413.   a. 1890s
414.   b. William Carney
415.   b. Republican Secretary of War Simon Cameron
416.   c. Approximately 15,000
417.   a. Benjamin O. Davis
418.   a. Poison Springs, Arkansas, April 18, 1864
419.   b. Established the Freedmen's Bureau

Women on Both Sides of the American Civil War: Nurses, Spies, and Soldiers

420.   a. Mary Edwards Walker
421.   a. Hundreds, though the exact number is unknown
422.   a. Belle Boyd
423.   d. Tailor
424.   d. Dorothea Lynde Dix
425.   a. Clara Barton
426.   d. All the above
427.   d. As a white male soldier
428.   b. Sally Louisa Tompkins
429.   d. Both B and C
430.   b. Richmond, Virginia
431.   b. Over 100
432.   d. Army
433.   a. Clara Barton
434.   d .1883
435.   c. Loreta Janeta Velazquez
436.   d. 400-1,000
437.   c. Vivandieres
438.   a. Susie King Taylor
439.   a. Mary Edwards Walker

Reconstruction Period Following War

440.   c. 1865-1877
441.   b. Reunite the North and South into a unified country
442.   b. Farm workers who leased land from planters
443.   d. All the above
444.   a. Ulysses S. Grant
445.   d. The Ten Percent Plan
446.   d. Two thousand
447.   a. Politicians who supported civil rights for African Americans
448.   d. All the above
449.   d. None of the above
450.   d. All the above
451.   b. Three
452.   b. Expansion of voting rights to all men
453.   a. Frederick Douglass
454.   d. All the above
455.   d. All the above
456.   d. All the above
457.   b. Forming paramilitary groups
458.   a. With the occupation of federal troops in those states
459.   a. It permitted federal troops to leave Southern states

Assassination of President Lincoln

460.   a. John Wilkes Booth
461.   a. April
462.   a. Ford's Theatre
463.   a. Andrew Johnson
464.   b. Three
465.   a. Gun
466.   a. Maryland
467.   a. Garret's Farm
468.   a. April 26, 1865
469.   d. Eight
470.   d. Four
471.   d. Both B and C
472.   a. Tom Taylor

473. d. Upon learning of Abraham Lincoln's death
474. a. Mary Todd Lincoln
475. a. "Sic semper tyrannis!"
476. a. Four years
477. b. Oak Ridge Cemetery, Illinois
478. d. A speech about Reconstruction and reunification
479. c. a military commission presided over by Major General David Hunter

Memorialization and Commemoration of the Civil War

480. c. The Soldiers' National Cemetery
481. d. All the above
482. b. Arlington National Cemetery
483. c. Grand Army of the Republic
484. d. African American Civil War Memorial
485. d. All the above
486. c. The Wall of Honor
487. d. Gettysburg
488. c. The Appomattox Monument
489. c. Decoration Day
490. b. Sons of Union Veterans of the Civil War
491. b. 427,981
492. a. 1865
493. a. Annual Commemoration of Surrender and Freedom Day
494. b. Arlington National Cemetery
495. d. The Missing Soldiers Office
496. b. Soldiers' & Sailors' Monument
497. b. 1868
498. d. All the above
499. c. The Civil War Unknowns Monument
500. d. Three

Check out another book in the series

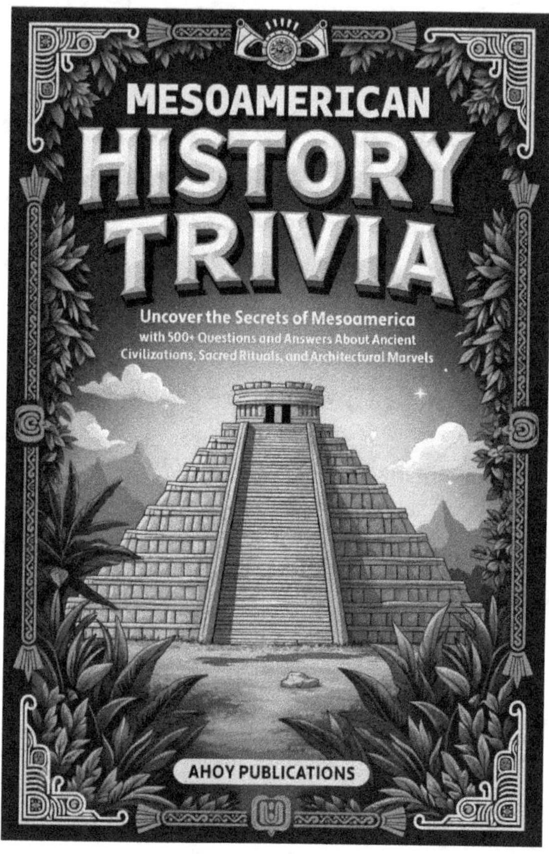

Welcome Aboard, Check Out This Limited-Time Free Bonus!

Ahoy, reader! Welcome to the Ahoy Publications family, and thanks for snagging a copy of this book! Since you've chosen to join us on this journey, we'd like to offer you something special.

Check out the link below for a FREE e-book filled with delightful facts about American History.

But that's not all - you'll also have access to our exclusive email list with even more free e-books and insider knowledge. Well, what are ye waiting for? Click the link below to join and set sail toward exciting adventures in American History.

Access your bonus here

https://ahoypublications.com/

Or, Scan the QR code!

* 9 7 9 8 8 9 2 9 6 5 5 6 9 *